# AFRICA IN THE MODERN WORLD

*Edited by* GWENDOLEN M. CARTER
*Indiana University, Bloomington*

The Cameroon Federal Republic
*by Victor T. Le Vine*

Dahomey: Between Tradition and Modernity
*by Dov Ronen*

Ethiopia: The Modernization of Autocracy
*by Robert L. Hess*

Liberia: The Evolution of Privilege
*by J. Gus Liebenow*

Rhodesia: Racial Conflict or Coexistence?
*by Patrick O'Meara*

West Africa's Council of the Entente
*by Virginia Thompson*

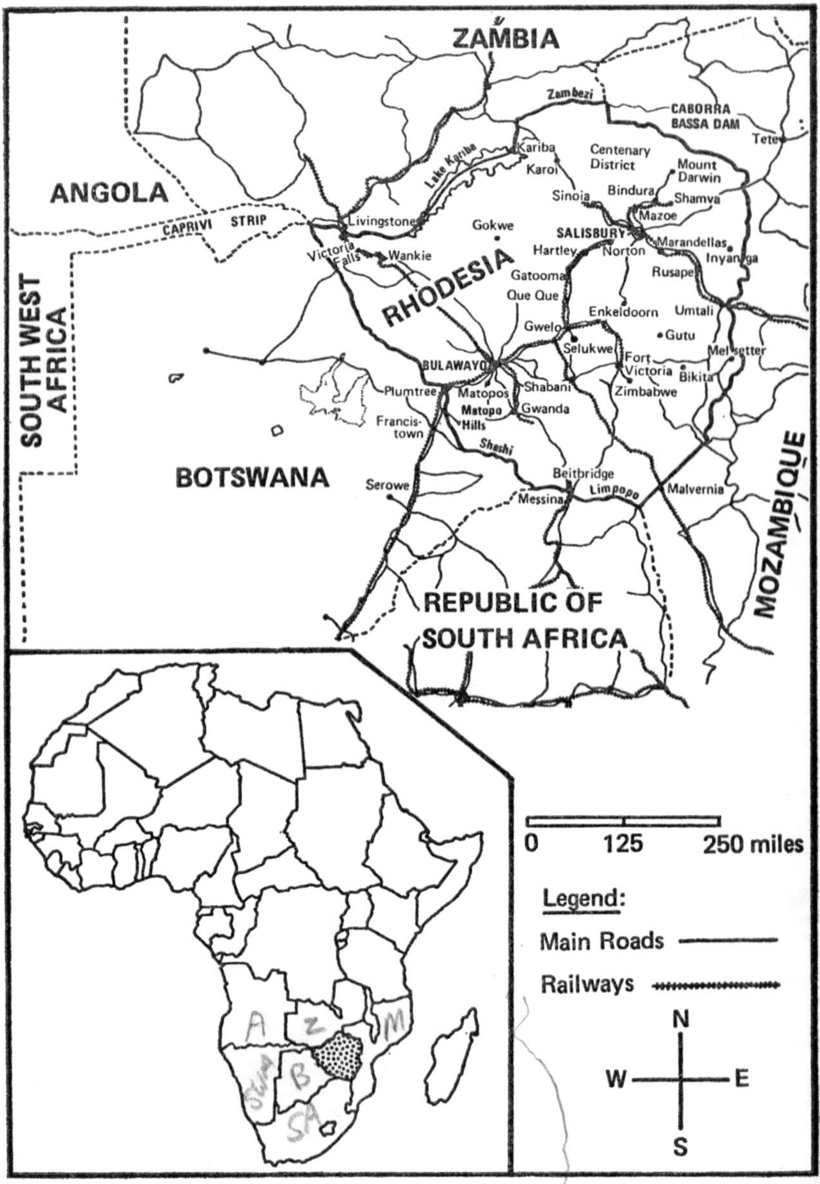


*Map 1.* Rhodesia

# RHODESIA

## Racial Conflict or Coexistence?

PATRICK O'MEARA
INDIANA UNIVERSITY

Cornell University Press
ITHACA AND LONDON

First published 1975 by Cornell University Press.
Published in the United Kingdom by Cornell University Press Ltd.,
2-4 Brook Street, London W1Y 1AA.

International Standard Book Number 0-8014-0923-3
Library of Congress Catalog Card Number 74-27442

Printed in the United States of America by Vail-Ballou Press, Inc.

To my parents,
who in so many ways
transcended the society
in which they lived

# Foreword

The historic slogan of the Pan African movement—"No African is truly free until all Africans live under governments of their own choice"—still rings throughout Africa. Nowhere has it had more meaning than among the nearly forty million Africans in southern Africa who have so long been dominated by white minority and colonial governments. Outside Africa, the plight of these Africans has also caused deep concern, for discrimination based on color is perhaps the most emotion-laden issue of our era.

What brought Rhodesia to the center of this concern has been the attempt by the small white minority to perpetuate its control over the African 95 per cent of the population through a constitutional *coup d'état.* In 1966 the Rhodesian government rejected the British demand that it guarantee specific provisions for African political advance as a prerequisite for being granted independence, and tried to acquire this status through its own unilateral declaration. But no country, not even South Africa and Portugal, has recognized its independence. Moreover, on the request of the British government, the United Nations has voted overwhelmingly a progressive series of economic sanctions against Rhodesia to force its government to concede African political advance. Thus the situation in Rhodesia has become a significant international issue, both because of United Nations action and even more because of the country's pivotal position regarding relations between white minorities and black majorities in southern Africa.

Sanctions against Rhodesia, although applied unevenly, have contributed to the pressures on behalf of African political rights. But more significant in determining the future direction of events have inevitably been the attitudes and actions of the African majority inside Rhodesia and of liberation groups based outside. The former openly demonstrated to the British Pearce Commission their opposition to modified settlement terms proposed by the British and Rhodesian governments that would have involved temporary material advantages but put off African majority rule into the distant future. Subsequent behind-the-scenes negotiations between the African National Council headed by Bishop Abel Muzorewa and the Ian Smith government have not achieved any agreed basis for constitutional advance. In any case, the meaningfulness of such discussions is being undercut by the striking successes of Rhodesian liberation groups, notably the Zimbabwe African National Union (ZANU) using bases held in parts of Mozambique by the Front for Liberation of Mozambique (FRELIMO). As the latter territory moves swiftly toward independence under a FRELIMO-dominated government, both external and internal pressures on the Rhodesian white regime will steadily increase.

The subtitle of this book, "Racial Conflict or Coexistence," spells out the limits within which African politics have been able to function in southern Africa. It is particularly in Rhodesia that the widest range of political approaches have been made by Africans. Some Africans have functioned inside the political system through political parties led by Africans or whites. Others have attempted to exert pressure for more political rights and other advantages through mass organizations working inside the country. The first groups, although they still play a tenuous role within the legislature, are increasingly stamped as collaborators and are losing whatever prestige and influence they had among their fellow Africans. Of the second group, persistent bannings and imprisonments drove earlier organizations underground or out of the country to engage in liberation efforts through appeals to Pan-African or world public opinion and ultimately through violence. While there are still African representatives in the Rhodesian legislature—and in recent years the African National Council under Bishop Muzorewa has taken up the challenge of pressure politics within the country—the spotlight increasingly turns on the externally based liberation groups attempting through violence to achieve change.

It is the particular merit of this work that Patrick O'Meara goes beyond a mere description of these different forms of pressure politics to set them within a frame of analysis based on conflict theory. Because African politics related to Rhodesia are considered as a part of a wide field of political analysis, this book contributes a useful perspective on a complex racial situation.

GWENDOLEN M. CARTER

# Acknowledgments

I would like to express my gratitude to a number of people who have either directly or indirectly helped me with this manuscript. I am particularly indebted to J. Gus Liebenow, professor of political science at Indiana University, whose guidance, patience, and inspiration make the study of Africa a challenging and worthwhile experience. Gwendolen Carter's keen insight into the problems of southern Africa and expert editorial guidance have immeasurably improved the quality of this book. I very much appreciate the hospitality and friendship extended to me by black and white Rhodesians on my numerous visits to that country, and by Rhodesian expatriates in Zambia and the United States. The resources made available to me by the University of Rhodesia, the *Rhodesia Herald,* the National Archives of Rhodesia, and the Library of Parliament proved invaluable.

Rebecca Kolkmeyer, Gail Sweetland, and Lilian Wunsch provided editorial and research assistance, and I am grateful to them. Finally, the generous support of the African Studies Program and the Office of Research and Advanced Studies at Indiana University greatly facilitated my research.

PATRICK O'MEARA

*Bloomington, Indiana*

# Contents

INTRODUCTION

# Toward a Framework for the Analysis of Rhodesian Politics

This book examines the contemporary black-white cleavage in Rhodesia, a cleavage between a white minority with political power and an African majority with minimum political controls and influence at its disposal. While the main focus is on current politics, the first chapter reviews the emergence and development of racial attitudes from 1890 onward. Specifically, the question is asked why some Africans accepted the ground rules of the Rhodesian political system, including laws, elections, and parliamentary norms and rewards, while others went beyond prescribed limits and sought the destruction of the system.

Political opposition crystallizes in several different ways: It may operate strictly within a defined political system as constitutional opposition, or it may be anomic, seeking the spontaneous resolution of grievances. It may seek to modify, transform, or destroy a system from within, or it may operate from without, as extrasystem opposition. In Rhodesia, Africans have attempted all of these approaches in recent years, but as yet without success.

At first, the African nationalist movements participated in system politics; currently they engage in extrasystem conflict. The organizations of the 1920's and 1930's, such as the Rhodesian Native Association and the Rhodesian Bantu Voters' Association, operated within a constitutional framework. Subsequently the African National Congress

(ANC) and the National Democratic Party (NDP) attempted to bring about radical but constitutional change within the system. But from the 1950's both the attitudes and actions of some nationalists were moving toward antisystem politics and then toward extrasystem conflict. Because of the intransigence of the white power structure, the Zimbabwe African People's Union (ZAPU) and Zimbabwe African National Union (ZANU) shifted from constitutional opposition to extrasystem political conflict—a qualitatively different political genre. From 1965 onward, however, other Africans participated in parliamentary opposition parties, such as the United People's Party, the National People's Union, and the Centre Party. These groups operated strictly within the political system of observed constitutional limitations.

The emergence of the African National Council in 1971 marked a temporary return to constitutional politics by some nationalist leaders (mainly from ZANU) in association with Africans within Rhodesia who were spontaneously responding to immediate and widespread fears that a settlement detrimental to their interests would be made between Great Britain and the Rhodesian Front government. At this time the return to a constitutional approach was precipitated by the British Pearce Commission's investigatory visit to Rhodesia, rather than by the nationalists' desire to compete within the existing political framework. The external presence of Great Britain, a responsible outside power attempting to divest itself of its responsibility but at the same time to protect both minority and majority interests, was once again a crucial variable in Rhodesian politics.

More precise distinctions may be drawn among political

competition, political opposition, and opposition of principle. Political competition involves a challenge of personnel, for example, in-party disputes over leadership. Political opposition indicates a difference over policy goals but a willingness to operate within a system, as was the case with African parliamentary opposition parties. This category covers a wide range of parties, from those to the far right of the Rhodesian Front to liberal white opposition. On the other hand, opposition of principle is a challenge to the continued existence of the system itself, what Otto Kirchheimer calls the desire for a degree of goal displacement incompatible with the constitutional requirements of a given system.[1]

Opposition of the first two types operates within a highly institutionalized political system that defines the different legal means of competition. An opposition that realizes it has a reasonable chance to assume governmental responsibility is likely to operate within, and strongly support, the prevailing system. But in Rhodesia, constitutional provisions providing Africans with meaningful opportunities for assuming governmental responsibility have not existed. Thus it was never likely that nationalist-minded Africans would strongly support the system. Even when they were prepared to operate within it, accepting Giovanni Sartori's view that "an opposition must oppose but not obstruct; it must be constructive not disruptive," [2] the more articulate Africans ultimately stamped working within the system as a form of collaboration.

[1] Otto Kirchheimer, "Germany, the Vanishing Opposition," in *Political Opposition in Western Democracies,* Robert Dahl, ed. (New Haven: Yale University Press, 1966), p. 237.

[2] Giovanni Sartori, "Opposition and Control: Problems and Prospects," *Government and Opposition,* 1, no. 2 (Feb. 1966), 151.

Some opposition groups, of course, diverge considerably from the traditional Western opposition models such as those of Britain and the United States, which center around an agreement to play fair (despite occasional aberrations) and acknowledge the rules of the parliamentary process as the permanent basis of the country's political life.[3] Patterns and styles of opposition may vary from system to system, while uniform operational codes or rules of the game remain. On the other hand, "an opposition may represent interests . . . in a way that is hardly conducive to checking absolute power vis-à-vis minorities and dissenting opinions. . . . Its primary role may be confined to providing a channel of information which actually lacks, in the final analysis, effectiveness and efficacy; or it may only be a safety valve, a merely verbal outlet, in the sense that opposition is tolerated only to placate opposition." [4] But even where opposition is tolerated only to placate discontent, as has been the case in Rhodesia, it still operates within and sustains the system.

The term "party" usually implies the coexistence of different competing entities and the inclusion of these as parts in a political whole—something that never genuinely existed in Rhodesia. It has been said that "only where the specific interests of parties are embedded in a common whole does the political struggle not lead to disintegration of the entire group." [5] Thus a stable political system should be based on a field of commonality or of

[3] See Silvano Tosi, "Italy: Anti-System Opposition within the System," *Government and Opposition,* 2, no. 1 (Nov. 1966), 49.

[4] Sartori, "Opposition and Control," pp. 149–150.

[5] Sigmund Neumann, *Modern Political Parties: Approaches to Comparative Parties* (Chicago: University of Chicago Press, 1965), p. 396.

consent on fundamentals. By its participation, a party actively creates conditions for its own survival and that of the system within which it operates.[6] In Rhodesia, the African parliamentary opposition parties and the Rhodesian Front Party share a commonality or consent on fundamentals. They both participate in the system and support it, seeking to change it from within.

Ideally there are three separate entities in a parliamentary system. The first is the party—a team of men seeking to control the governing apparatus by gaining office in a duly constituted election. It has a unique history and a constellation of alternatives which it presents to the electorate. The party operates on several different levels: it seeks the selection of personnel, the formulation of public policies, the conducting or criticizing of government, political education, intervention between the individual and the government; representation, conversion, aggregation (i.e., compromise between competing points of view); integration (i.e., participation, socialization, and mobilization); persuasion, recruitment, and choice of leaders; policy formation; and control of government. The second entity is the opposition party (or parties), and the third is the political system in which both operate. While the requisites for constitutional politics include the existence of a shared political community (which transcends the issues over which the contestants battle) and a relatively stable and pluralistic balance between various social groups (with political resources to defend their interests), a form of con-

[6] Roy C. Macridis, "Introduction: The History, Function, and Typology of Parties," in *Political Parties, Contemporary Trends and Ideas,* Roy C. Macridis, ed. (New York: Harper Torchbooks, 1967), p. 19.

flict is not excluded from the system.[7] Indeed, the conflict-integration dialectic is central to an understanding of the operation of parties within a political system; conflict frequently helps to revitalize existent norms, or it contributes to the emergence of new norms. In this sense, social conflict is a mechanism for adjustment of norms to those adequate to new conditions. Clearly, then, an institutionalized form of conflict serves a constructive end by translating issues into objectives which can be achieved within the system.

In Rhodesia conflict of this type, leading to reaffirmation of the system or the integration of change, has primarily occurred within white politics. Since the Unilateral Declaration of Independence in 1965, however, even this dimension has been limited. Opposition challenging the Rhodesian Front Party has been regarded as a threat to the viability of the system. On the other hand, the Rhodesian Front Party has attempted to integrate opposition to its right, or from the right wing within the party itself.

The question that now arises is why some conflicts may be categorized as institutionalized party conflicts operating through regularized channels, while others move out of this orbit, as has happened in Rhodesia. In order to understand this problem better, a distinction must be drawn between political opposition and political conflict: "Constitutional opposition presupposes 'quiet politics,' not turbulent politics. . . . Constitutional opposition belongs to a peaceful view of politics, not to a war-like approach in which the opposer is an enemy, an *hostis*." [8] The system,

[7] See Lewis Coser, *The Functions of Social Conflict* (Glencoe, Ill.: Free Press, 1964), p. 154.

[8] Sartori, "Opposition and Control," p. 151.

then, is one in which conflict serves a functional rather than a dysfunctional role and in which procedures exist for the management of conflict. It is one with channels for protest and scope for mobilization.

Political conflict, however, arises when such channels for pressure are seen to be inadequate or are believed to hamper particular objectives. At that point the issue becomes the extent or character of protest or conflict. Various factors affect the severity or intensity of political conflict: the composition of the groups engaged in the conflict, the readiness or reluctance of the incumbents of political power to broaden bases of support within that system, the scope of representation, the role of pressure groups, and the feasibility of alliances. In a plural society where the same persons are opponents on one occasion and allies on another, conflicts are likely to be less severe than in a situation where the lines are more permanently and rigidly drawn, as in Rhodesia. The severity of a conflict also depends on the way in which one conflict is related to another.[9] It is possible for conflict to take place along different lines of cleavage—ideological, religious, ethnic, and so on. Where these factors reinforce each other, as in part they do in Rhodesia, the conflict tends to intensify. Conflicts may be further subdivided according to: scale—the degree of threatened disruption; scope—the size of the units involved; pervasiveness—the number and kinds of relationships disrupted; duration; and, finally, manifest expression—the specific overt activities involved.

Certain types of conflict may cut across society and unify different groups; for example, as we shall see, in a racial

[9] See Robert A. Dahl, *Pluralist Democracy in the United States* (Chicago: Rand McNally, 1967), p. 271.

conflict between white and black, some cross-cutting alignments may emerge as white groups join in common cause with Africans, although in Rhodesia the struggle is essentially a polarized one. Structurally, these groups may be united by commonly accepted definitions of their aims and the means by which these aims are to be achieved. In such groups, actions by members may convey specific meaning to other members, reflecting either irrelevance, assistance, or opposition. One of the primary aims may be group cohesion—the continued struggle with the outside may necessitate an intolerance of internal opposition.

A conflict involving high stakes frequently has no solutions other than the "mutually incompatible kind." [10] Conflict may become revolutionary, where one class of people comes to believe that the only solution to their problem lies in the destruction of the prevailing system. When ideological differences are so sharp that a meeting point may never be possible, recognition by one of the groups of the fundamental irreconcilability of the division may be the only way to create basic change. African nationalists have increasingly moved in this direction. Although white liberals and some Africans working within the system have also explored the solution of coexistence, fundamental change by constitutional means—such as a move from a white minority political system to one that responds to majority interests—is remote. Evidence that a conflict is growing more severe would include harsher language, in which opponents are portrayed as implacable enemies to be annihilated; greater stress on actual employment of violence against opponents; and an increased resort to means

[10] *Ibid.*

that were previously regarded as illegitimate or unconstitutional. This latter criterion is an important one—the decision to move out of the context of a given system and into an uncharted area of extrasystem opposition with all of its implications of violence and revolutionary change. However sharp the initial distinctions between groups may have been, they may deepen as the out-group develops holistic ideological beliefs that attempt to rationalize and explain its actions. Creating such legitimacy is an important variable; before the hostile attitudes of the out-group, or negatively privileged group, can be turned into action, the group must develop the awareness that it is indeed negatively privileged. It must come to believe that it is being denied rights to which it is entitled. It must reject any justification for the existing distribution of rights, and privileges.[11] The conflicting parties then no longer share the basic values or consensual bases of the system, and the result is "a struggle over values and claims to scarce status, power and resources in which the aims of the opponents are to neutralize, injure or eliminate their rivals." [12]

Conflict situations may be resolved in different ways: by annihilation of one group, by total or partial compliance by one group based on the realization that continuation of the conflict would be futile, and, finally, by compromise or mutual concessions, a recognition that opposing forces are not always equal or complementary, nor are they always likely to become so. In any of these events, a relatively extensive and enduring reordering and redefining of the process of social organization is the end re-

[11] Coser, *Social Conflict,* p. 137. [12] *Ibid.,* p. 8.

sult. If the balance of power is stable after an agreement, common norms might develop for the behavior of members of both groups. Possibly, however, only an uneasy compliance will result, with both sides prepared to resume the conflict.

# RHODESIA

## Racial Conflict or Coexistence?

CHAPTER 1

# From White Settlement to Unilateral Declaration of Independence: A Historical Overview

Rhodesia [1] lies on the northern edge of white-controlled Africa between Zambia (formerly Northern Rhodesia) in the north and the Transvaal (in the Republic of South Africa) in the south. It is bounded to the east by Mozambique, and to the west by independent, African-ruled Botswana (the former British protectorate of Bechuanaland). Rhodesia covers an area of 150,333 squares miles, approximately the size of California; its 271,000 [2] whites dominate its 5,700,000 Africans,[3] although the latter outnumber them by twenty to one.

Between 1890 and 1965, Rhodesian history falls into five pivotal periods: white settlement and the rule of the British South Africa Company, responsible government, the Central African Federation, the 1961 constitution, and, finally, the circumstances surrounding the Unilateral Declaration of Independence (UDI) in 1965. Several dis-

1 Until the promulgation of the 1965 constitution, the country was referred to as Southern Rhodesia.

2 *Economic Survey of Rhodesia for 1973* (Salisbury: Government Publications Office, 1973), Table 10, p. 17.

3 The proportion of Mashona (Shona) to Ndebele (Matabele) is approximately 11 : 3.

tinct motifs underlie and link each of the periods: the uncertain constitutional status of the country, the significance of the external presence of Great Britain, the use of the franchise to sustain white minority privilege and political control and to perpetuate chronic African disadvantage.

Two archetypical colonial figures dominate white Rhodesian history: David Livingstone, missionary,[4] humanitarian, and liberator; and Cecil Rhodes, empire builder. Livingstone felt that "Christianity and commerce" would free Africans from ignorance, disease, the slave trade, and famine. Rhodes, however, saw central Africa as a strategic area for both personal and British imperial involvement. He had heard of the extensive ruins of Zimbabwe, and, in particular, that gold existed there.[5] Despite the fact that the ancient workings had been abandoned, it was well known that gold had once been mined by the Rozwi people, and in the era of the Transvaal gold boom, the possibility of future gold deposits could not be overlooked. Central Africa was also considered a vital link in a direct line of British possessions between the Cape and Cairo.

[4] The London Missionary Society encouraged Livingstone's explorations between 1851 and 1873, and in 1859 set up a mission in Zambesia, as Southern Rhodesia was called.

[5] The Zimbabwe ruins near the town of Fort Victoria have both historical and symbolic importance. Most white Rhodesians refuse to see the modern Shona as descendants of the Rozwi people who built Zimbabwe, since Zimbabwe implies African achievement and civilization. Africans however, have regarded Zimbabwe as their "Golden Age" and named two of their nationalist movements after it: the Zimbabwe African People's Union and the Zimbabwe African National Union. They already refer to the country as Zimbabwe, and it will be so called when it becomes independent under African control.

## *The British South Africa Company*

Rhodes first began to make plans for opening up the region in 1878, but not until 1888 (following Portugal's claim in 1887 to all of the interior between Angola on the Atlantic coast and Mozambique on the Indian Ocean) did he feel it was time for him to act. He was motivated by a combination of personal gain, the concerns of empire, and the pressures of the Portuguese. His agents immediately attempted to obtain treaties from Lobengula, the king of the Ndebele. The Rudd Mineral Concession, granted by Lobengula in 1888 (but later repudiated by him), gave Rhodes a monopoly for the mining of minerals throughout the Ndebele kingdom.

In 1889, Rhodes and his associates obtained a royal charter to form the British South Africa Company. The charter authorized the company "to settle and administer [an area] immediately to the north of the South African Republic and west of the Portuguese Dominions." [6]

In 1890 a pioneer column consisting of two hundred settlers and five hundred police reached the site of the future capital of Rhodesia, Fort Salisbury. The arrival of the white settlers marks the beginning of the period of sustained conflict between white and black in Southern Rhodesia: a conflict between those with skills and western technology at their disposal, and the Africans with a minimal level of technology. The Rudd Concession had granted no rights of settlement or administration, but by bringing a strong military force into Mashonaland, where the African population was sparse and Lobengula's authority was

[6] Great Britain C. 8773, *Charter of the British South Africa Company* (Oct. 29, 1889).

intermittent, the company succeeded in establishing the first European settlement at Salisbury in 1890 and appointed an administrator of Mashonaland.[7] Lobengula was deeply disturbed, and on August 10, 1889, he wrote to Queen Victoria: "The white people are troubling me much about gold. If you have heard that I have given my whole country to Rhodes, it is not my words. I have not done so, Rhodes wants to take my country by strength." [8] Indeed, there then followed the "pacification" of the Ndebele and Shona peoples.

The Ndebele rose in rebellion and were first defeated in 1893. In 1896 they rebelled again and were once again defeated. Lobengula had fled after the first defeat and subsequently died. The company refused to recognize any successor in his place so as to prevent the re-emergence of a strong centralized kingdom. Acting independently from the Ndebele, the Shona also rebelled and were defeated between 1896 and 1897. Although the Africans were eliminated as immediate and real combatants and the whites assumed an assured control, thereafter the whites had greater respect (though a respect based on fear) for both the Shona and the Ndebele.

In the light of the uprisings and under pressure from the white settlers, who wanted to have an active role in the formulation of policies and goals for Southern Rhodesia, Rhodes agreed to accelerate the grant of representative government.[9] In 1898 a Legislative Council was created

[7] For a further discussion see Colin Leys, *European Politics in Southern Rhodesia* (Oxford: Clarendon Press, 1959), p. 5.

[8] Quoted in Philip Mason, *The Birth of a Dilemma* (London: Oxford University Press, 1958), pp. 144–145.

[9] Because of Rhodes's participation in the Jameson Raid in 1895 (a badly planned attempt to forcibly take the control of the gold-

with five appointed and four popularly elected members.

Up to 1908 the British South Africa Company controlled the council by maintaining its officials in a majority. But in that year, while retaining control over the executive, the company relinquished its majority. By 1913 the elected majority was raised to two-thirds in a council of eighteen. The electoral qualifications were similar to those in operation at the Cape at this time. Based on income and property ownership, they reflected Rhodes's now famous maxim of "equal rights for all civilized men irrespective of race, south of the Zambezi," although his criteria for civilization were clearly of a dubious nature. The effect was an overwhelmingly white electorate.

By 1904 there were 12,000 settlers in Rhodesia, and by 1911 the white population was nearly 24,000 and was primarily engaged in one form of agriculture or another. The Europeans preferred the higher and healthier country, and so the High Veld came to be predominantly inhabited by Europeans.[10] In the Middle Veld (to the north and south of the High Veld), African reserves and European-owned farms intermingled. In the Low Veld (the unhealthy malarial area of sparse rainfall), European settlement was almost completely absent.

For the first fifteen years of its rule, the British South Africa Company felt that the eventual output of gold would justify its large investment for administration and development, such as building expensive railroads into

---

rich Transvaal out of the hands of the Boers) and because of the uprisings and settler discontent in Rhodesia, both the British public and the British government felt that there was a need for considerable reform in southern Africa.

[10] European settlement was also influenced by the location of the railway, which gave white farmers access to markets.

Portuguese East Africa and South Africa. But the company had grossly overestimated the wealth of central Africa and obtained little profit from its struggling settlement. In addition, there were frequent disputes with the settlers, who felt that their interests were secondary to profits. Nonetheless, when the twenty-five-year term of the British South Africa Company's charter expired in 1914, the settlers chose to support the continuation of the charter rather than to join the Union of South Africa or to press for self-government. The British government then renewed the charter for ten years.

### *Responsible Government*

In 1921 a royal commission, the Buxton Commission, was appointed to examine the possibility of responsible government and a new constitution for Rhodesia. It suggested a referendum among the whites on the same three possibilities: the continuation of the British South Africa Company rule (which was still universally disliked), union with South Africa, or self-government.

There was much to be said for the incorporation of Southern Rhodesia into the Union. The country had been colonized largely from the south; its law was fundamentally the same as that of the Cape (both were based on Roman Dutch law); there was a continuous railway between the two countries, and Southern Rhodesia's trade was mainly with the towns and ports of South Africa. The majority, however, fearing too close an alliance with the Afrikaners of South Africa, voted in favor of self-government.[11] Rho-

[11] F. M. G. Willson, ed. (*Source Book of Parliamentary Elections and Referenda in Southern Rhodesia, 1898–1962* [Salisbury: Univer-

desia had emerged as a national entity, and this factor, coupled with a fear of social and economic integration, contributed to the rejection of incorporation with South Africa. Thus company rule was dissolved, and Rhodesia was formally annexed to the British Crown since it had never been a formal colonial possession of Great Britain. Chronologically, a missionary presence had been followed by commercial entrepreneurs backed by force and finally by the British Crown.

Under the constitution of 1923, a Crown-appointed governor acted on the advice of Rhodesian ministers except in regard to certain legislation—for example, legislation pertaining to discrimination against the "indigenous population," over which the British government retained a right of veto. As Sir Roy Welensky put it: "The British government has never had the power unless they were prepared to use the sword. They have never had the power to force anything on Rhodesia." [12]

Although the British had power only to prohibit, they did restrain the Rhodesian government from introducing certain racial legislation. The existence of the reserve powers maintained the nonracial character of the electoral roll and preserved some individual freedoms in Rhodesia.

In 1923, Southern Rhodesia was something of a political

---

sity College of Rhodesia and Nyasaland, Department of Government, 1963], p. 115), gives these statistics for November 7, 1922:

| | |
|---|---|
| Total electorate | 18,810 |
| Total effective votes | 14,763 |
| Percentage poll | 78.48 |
| Pro responsible government | 8,774 (59.4%) |
| Pro union | 5,989 (40.6%) |
| Majority in favor of responsible government | 2,785 |

12 Interview, Salisbury, July 1967.

anomaly—a self-governing colony controlled in practice by its small white minority. The Legislative Assembly consisted of thirty members and the cabinet was composed of seven members. Although there was what might be referred to as a "colorblind franchise" similar to that of the earlier Cape Colony—voters were qualified by age, nationality, and an annual income of over £200—few Africans could meet these conditions.

The obvious geographical unity of the three central African territories of Southern Rhodesia, Northern Rhodesia, and Nyasaland led to discussions, after 1924, of the possibility of some form of political union between them. Having turned away from South Africa, Southern Rhodesia now turned toward Nyasaland and Northern Rhodesia. The ratio of whites to Africans in southern, eastern, and central Africa differed widely; Kenya, 1 to 100; Northern Rhodesia, 1 to 50; Southern Rhodesia, 1 to 20; South Africa, 1 to 4. The Hilton-Young Commission of 1929, which investigated the possibility of closer relations between the three areas, stressed "the paramountcy of native interests." [13] This statement was in keeping with changing conceptions of what British policy should be in both east and central Africa, for it particularly concerned the small white minority in Northern Rhodesia, and they now looked to the whites of Southern Rhodesia for solidarity.

In Southern Rhodesia the victory of Godfrey Huggins (later Lord Malvern) and his United Party in 1933 reflected a similar concern. Huggins was a pivotal figure in central African politics from 1933 to 1956. By the late 1930's, Huggins and his party had evolved their policy of

[13] Great Britain Cmd. 3234 (1929), *The Commission on Closer Union of Dependencies in East and Central Africa.*

"a double pyramid."[14] This approach stressed the separate development of the races with their ultimate meeting, though in the distant future, on the national level. To implement this policy, the government accentuated in their legislation the separate areas for development of the different racial groups. The Land Apportionment Act of 1930 (recommended by the Morris Carter Commission) excluded Africans from permanent rights to land in European areas and reserved less than half of the colony's land for Africans.[15] The Industrial Conciliation Act of 1934 created a color bar to entrance to skilled employment.

Huggins was aware that the British would be reluctant to grant independence to a territory under minority control and saw advantages to Southern Rhodesia through some form of amalgamation with Northern Rhodesia and Nyasaland. The copper resources of Northern Rhodesia and the African labor reservoir of Nyasaland were particular incentives to such a move.

A conference held between Northern and Southern Rho-

[14] By the late 1940's, Huggins had publicly moved away from the "double pyramid" policy, although many of its principles remained embedded in Rhodesian thought and political action.

[15] C.S.R. 3-1926, *Report of the Land Commission.* The Southern Rhodesian Native Reserves were defined in the Letters Patent of the 1923 constitution. Close to 21 million acres were set aside for African use and occupation; the most favorable land was set aside for white use. In some ways this protected Africans from the encroaching white settlement, but it also produced a polarized landholding system. The Land Apportionment Act (1941) established the Special Native Area exclusively for Africans. The 1961 constitution set up Tribal Trust Lands which expanded the Reserves by 19 million acres. By the end of 1966, Tribal Trust Lands were 40,020,000 acres of a total Rhodesian area of 96,600,000 acres. The Land Tenure Act of 1969 redivided Rhodesia into two parts: 45 million acres for Africans and 45 million for whites.

desia at the Victoria Falls in 1935 requested the appointment of a commission to study the possibility of amalgamation. In 1939 the British Bledisloe Commission accepted amalgamation "in principle" but deferred any final position on the matter because it felt that the discriminatory policies of Southern Rhodesia would clash with Britain's commitment to the Africans in Northern Rhodesia.

*The Central African Federation*

Shortly before the end of World War II, Huggins once again took up the idea of federation. Despite opposition to amalgamation by white Southern Rhodesians, who feared that the greatly increased proportion of Africans to whites in such a federation might bring about "the Gold Coast ideas" of African domination, there had been a subtle change in white Rhodesian thinking. Economic development and urbanization made complete separation less attractive for Rhodesians. The growing interdependence of black and white necessarily modified the "two-pyramid" scheme. In essence, while political control must remain in white hands, black-white interaction on an economic and a limited social level was not to be excluded from consideration.

The Central African Federation came into being in 1953 as a result of urging by whites in both Southern and Northern Rhodesia and the compliance of the British Conservative government.[16] But as the decade moved on, the rate of progress toward multiracialism both in the Federation and in Southern Rhodesia became an issue of concern. The key word in the political vocabulary of the

[16] The federal concept, however, had been initiated under a Labour government.

Federation was "partnership." [17] For Huggins, this term was "a very blessed word" and is said to have described what Huggins considered "partnership of the [black] horse and the [white] rider." [18] For the British government it implied ultimate equality for the Africans. For most Africans, it meant a still uncertain future.

In the Southern Rhodesian political sphere, Huggins's move into federal politics in 1953 resulted in the election of a new prime minister, Garfield Todd, a former missionary from New Zealand. In the context of white Rhodesian politics, Todd stands out as the only prime minister who moved beyond what he once referred to as "the white enclave mentality." [19] While, albeit under his leadership, the legislature in Southern Rhodesia was passing laws such as the restrictive Public Order Act (which authorized troops to break up strikes), Todd was at the same time contemplating innovations which alarmed the majority of his own United Federal Party: "Several of us went over this bridge to work from within Garfield Todd's party. By 1956 a stage had been reached when Africans had begun to regard the government as their own. African activity in the UFP was not extensive, but it was effective." [20] In 1956 he appointed Sir Robert Tredgold to head a commission to reconsider the whole question of franchise rights. In the same year the Dominion Party was founded, the predeces-

[17] Great Britain Cmnd. 1148 (1960), *Report of the Advisory Commission of the Review of the Constitution of Rhodesia and Nyasaland.*

[18] T. R. H. Creighton, *The Anatomy of Partnership* (London: Faber and Faber, 1960), pp. 104–105.

[19] Quoted in T. Franck, *Race and Nationalism* (New York: Fordham University Press, 1960), p. 87.

[20] Quoted in Nathan M. Shamuyarira, *Crisis in Rhodesia* (London: Andre Deutsch, 1965), p. 21.

sor of the present Rhodesian Front Party, with white supremacist and antifederation policies.

The United Federal Party dominated the political scene with twenty-five of the thirty-five members of the Federal Legislative Assembly and twenty-four of the twenty-nine of the Southern Rhodesian Assembly. It had been formed by the merger in late 1957 of the Federal Party, led by Prime Minister Roy Welensky, and the United Rhodesia Party, led by Todd. The party made a point of encouraging African members, and in 1958 six of its branches were African, out of a total of 160.[21] In February 1958, Todd supported a revised franchise which would have ensured the voter registration of all Africans who had received ten years of education. In January 1958, the cabinet resigned for a number of reasons: the race issue, personality differences with Todd, and as a direct result of interference by federal cabinet ministers who were concerned about Todd's support for the federal framework. Todd did not follow customary parliamentary procedures but tried to remain in office and set up a new cabinet. In February 1958, a special party congress, in a stormy session, elected Sir Edgar Whitehead to replace Todd. Todd's potential for change had been curbed. The budding African expectations of an increasing share in the making of policy were abruptly ended.

## *The 1961 Constitution*

Sir Edgar Whitehead succeeded Todd as prime minister of Rhodesia at a time when the federal structure was break-

[21] Channing B. Richardson, "Central African Federation: New Step in Africa?" *Foreign Policy Bulletin,* May 1, 1958.

ing up. The British government's initial enthusiasm for the Federation was giving way to a growing realization that opposition within and outside central Africa was damaging its international image. Moreover, if internal opposition continued to grow, the only way to save the Federation might be by the use of force. Toward the end of 1960 the British Monckton Commission[22] held that no form of association between the three territories was likely to succeed unless Southern Rhodesia was willing to make drastic changes in its racial policies. From the other side, the right-wing Dominion Party in Southern Rhodesia, led by Winston Field, rejected further black-white compromises and renewed its demands for secession from the Federation and Dominion status for Southern Rhodesia alone. They determined "to establish in Central Africa a great nation." Maintaining that the fears of the earlier opponents of federation had been justified, they proposed to solve the problems of the white minority with a massive immigration scheme. In addition, they declared that Southern Rhodesia was no closer to independence than it had been in 1953 and that concessions to Africans had gone too far.

Sir Edgar Whitehead was well aware that the Federation had been of great value as an economic unity. Capital investment totaled more than £805,000,000 between 1954

[22] Members of the commission included Elspeth Huxley, writer on African affairs; D. T. Jack, professor of economics at the University of Durban; the Rev. R. H. W. Shepherd, moderator of the Church of Scotland; Justice Hugh Beadle, judge of the Rhodesian High Court; C. Ellman-Brown, chartered accountant, formerly a minister in the administration of Todd; and Simon Sigola, a chief from the Essexvale district.

and 1959. National income had risen from £303,000,000 in 1954 to £440,000,000 in 1959, and exports had increased 74 per cent. In addition the Kariba Dam had begun supplying electricity to major industrial centers in both Southern and Northern Rhodesia.

Nonetheless, Harold Macmillan's "wind of change" speech in Cape Town in early 1960 heralded a new era in African politics. He was responding to the clear demands for independence from the former British colonial possessions in East and West Africa. In January, Kenya received a new constitution that would lead to majority rule; in April, Hastings Banda, now president of Malawi, was released by the British authorities and began to reorganize his party in Nyasaland. In June the Congo became independent, and by November so had Nigeria, Togoland, the Cameroon, and all of French West Africa. At the same time, white refugees began to come into the Federation from the Congo, and the racial prejudices of white Rhodesians were beginning to harden.

In Southern Rhodesia the African attitude to federation was far from clear. The leaders of the National Democratic Party (NDP) were certainly against it, but there were Africans who thought it would be in the African interest to remain within a federation which would ultimately assume full self-determination, and with this in mind, they asked the Monckton Commission to transfer more functions, such as African education and labor, to the federal government. The Monckton Report recommended that "such constitutional changes as may be desirable in Southern Rhodesia should be negotiated and put into effect without awaiting the full revision of the federal structure."[23] Simply, then, Rhodesia was to put its constitutional house in order before the dissolution of the Federation. Since all groups in Southern Rhodesia were anxious for some clarification of the constitutional position, a series of constitutional meetings began in February 1961. It was hoped that somehow there could be a reconciliation between the African Nationalist demands for "one man–one vote" and the white attempts to restrict the franchise. As a result of these meetings, a new constitution was agreed upon and, at first, was accepted by the African Nationalists.

The new constitution created two voters' rolls, an A and a B roll, whose voting qualifications were based on financial and educational standards. Most whites were on the A roll, but the overwhelming proportion of Africans could get only on the B roll. Since there were fifty constituencies in which the A-roll electorate predominated and only fifteen electoral districts in which B-roll voters were in the majority, the general effect was to give A-roll voters control over the Legislative Assembly. Because of this fact, although the Nationalists had first accepted the constitution, they now rejected it. According to Enoch Dumbutshena, representative of the NDP in London, the rejection came after an examination of the implications of the new conditions of the franchise. The number of African children that passed form 2 in any one year, the potential number of African property buyers, the exclusion of property owned in the Trust lands, and the average African wage were all taken into consideration. More important than these was the fact that even if there were one hundred thousand African voters on the B roll, their votes

[23] Cmnd. 1148 (1960), *Report of the Advisory Commission*, p. 111.

would be confined to electing only fifteen members in a house of sixty-five.[24]

The 1961 constitution made it impossible for Africans to achieve majority rule for a great number of years, if ever.[25] Only about 608,000 of Southern Rhodesia's approximately 3,970,000 Africans were in paid employment in 1963, even less than the some 622,000 in mid-1962. The average African wage in 1964 was $315 a year, while the average white wage was approximately $3,300. The Africans had three choices in this period in pressing for change: to work through nonpolitical or quasi-political activity, such as the trade unions; to operate within the constitutional system; or to go outside of the system.[26] They might have welcomed the proposals if these had been introduced a few years earlier; by 1961 it was too little, too late. Sir Edgar Whitehead's government, while saying that it wanted greater African participation, saw African nationalism as a destructive force. Yet African nationalism was the very movement that attracted the greatest popular African support. In opposing it, the government was seen as the opponent, not the supporter, of African aspirations.

## *Toward a Unilateral Declaration of Independence*

But if the African Nationalists were unhappy about the new constitution, so too were many white rightists because

[24] Enoch Dumbutshena, "Why the Nationalists Rejected the 1961 Constitution," in *Southern Rhodesia: The Price of Freedom,* Fred B. Rea, ed. (Bulawayo, Rhodesia: Midrho Press, 1964), p. 77.

[25] See, for a more detailed discussion, Muriel Horrell, *Days of Crisis in Rhodesia* (Johannesburg: South African Institute of Race Relations, 1965), p. 1.

[26] See James P. Barber, *Rhodesia: The Road to Rebellion* (London: Oxford University Press, 1967), p. 6.

of the many liberal proposals that they saw built into it. European apprehension was primarily due to the realization that African participation in government was now at hand; they felt there would now be competition for jobs, and Africans would ask for rights to mix socially and to live in white areas. Sir Edgar Whitehead lost the 1962 election on this basis, and liberal reform came to an end. Following the election, the United Federal Party was disbanded and became the opposition Rhodesia Party.

A major reason for this result was that Africans who were eligible to vote refused to register despite an intensive "Build a Nation" campaign designed by Sir Edgar Whitehead's party. Less than one-quarter of the estimated 50,000 African electorate registered to vote because the Nationalists discouraged voting in the election. Sir Roy Welensky maintained:

> I personally feel rather strongly and deeply about the failure of the Nationalists to play a reasonable part here. They had a wonderful opportunity to do something in Rhodesia. I'll give you an example. In the election of '62 in the territorial field I was not responsible. I was Federal prime minister, as you know. Five seats, however, were lost in the Bulawayo area, which would have given my Party, in Rhodesia, a majority in the House and we would have won by their voting on instructions from their leaders. This would have opened the flood gates.[27]

The real importance of this election was that from then on African Nationalists began to move outside of the white political system. The real opposition was outside of the Southern Rhodesian Legislative Assembly if not out-

[27] Interview, July 1967. It is important to note that the Nationalists would have been willing to forego majority rule in favor of a "blocking third in the House," but this was not forthcoming.

side the country (i.e., nationalist groups in exile), and most serious of all, it was predominantly black.

One of the first acts of the new Rhodesian prime minister, Winston Field, was to take up negotiations with the new British Labour prime minister, Harold Wilson, on the future status of Rhodesia and, in particular, on the question of independence. In essence, the British conditions for granting independence were enumerated in five principles—the NIBMAR Principles: No Independence Before Majority African Rule—which were to become the stumbling block to all future negotiations. They were: (1) the principle of unimpeded progress toward majority rule; (2) guarantees against retrogressive amendments to the constitution to retard African advancement; (3) an immediate increase in political representation of Africans; (4) an end to racial discrimination; and (5) evidence to the satisfaction of the British government that any basis of independence was acceptable to the people of Rhodesia as a whole. To these five Wilson added a sixth in January 1966: assurance that, regardless of race, there was no oppression of the majority by the minority or the minority by the majority. For the Rhodesian Front government the British principles represented, not a basis for negotiations, but an ultimatum. In the words of Desmond Lardner-Burke, the minister of justice and law and order, the fundamental difference between the Rhodesian and the British governments was this: "the Rhodesians believe that the reins of government should be held in responsible hands." [28]

In 1963, the first year that the Rhodesian Front Party

[28] Desmond Lardner-Burke, *Rhodesia: History of the Crisis* (London: Oldbourne, 1966), p. 5.

was in power, the breakup of the Central African Federation and the granting of independence to Nyasaland (as Malawi) and Northern Rhodesia (as Zambia) was heralded. The ideology of the Rhodesian Front Party made any form of cooperation with black governments problematical. Southern Rhodesia had benefited considerably from the Federation, but the costs for the continued alliance were considered too high, leaving aside the question of whether or not the new black governments themselves wanted to continue the Federation. The breakup resulted in Southern Rhodesia's receiving many of the benefits of the Federation; for example, all federal military equipment was returned to it.

Within the year, Winston Field had been eased out as prime minister. In a prepared statement Field said that "serious disagreements had arisen between my Party, the House and myself, in relation to policy, and I have been requested to retire in order to make way for someone else." Ian Smith was in power, summoning the "Spirit of '96"—1896, the year in which the pioneers had defeated the Ndebele. Asked whether the party would be taking a firmer line on independence, Ian Smith replied: "I would have thought that we had been taking a fairly firm line all along. I think it has been said on numerous occasions that we have no intention of weakening on this question of independence. We will continue that way." [29] The government, he added, wanted a negotiated independence and would continue to strive for that, "but we have made it quite clear that we can visualise circumstances which might drive us to do something else." He denied that

[29] *Africa Research Bulletin,* April 14, 1964.

Field's retirement was in any way connected with the question of independence.

Smith urged white voters to prepare to fight physically for the maintenance of white supremacy in Rhodesia. Along more practical lines, he used the Law and Order (Maintenance) Act in order to restrict some 400 Africans without trial (i.e., they were not permitted to move from defined areas) and to detain more than 1,000 others.

The great obstacle to independence was the Wilson Labour government which had been elected in October 1964. White Rhodesians had long been suspicious of the British Labour Party, particularly since in the 1930's Labour had fostered the concept of "the paramountcy of native interests," which Rhodesians regarded as a betrayal. With Smith as prime minister, UDI, a Unilateral Declaration of Independence, became a definite possibility and not just a bargaining tool. There were many, including Sir Edgar Whitehead, who were alarmed at the prospect of such a drastic step and stressed the economic isolation that might follow such a declaration. Indeed, Whitehead's RP (Rhodesia Party) waged a vigorous campaign opposing any such declaration.

The referendum on the question of independence on the basis of the 1961 constitution gave Ian Smith a majority of 89 per cent, and in a general election in May 1965 the Rhodesian Front Party won all 50 A-roll seats. Smith now had a solid basis of public, albeit white public, support for leverage in negotiating with Britain. He also claimed after the Domboshawa Indaba (a council or meeting of chiefs) that he had the solid support of the African chiefs. Following the 1965 election, Whitehead's RP was eliminated. However, Africans elected to the Legislative Assembly on the B roll came together to form the United People's Party—thirteen parliamentarians elected with a total of less than 800 votes.

With the backing of a highly organized party, which had won national elections in 1962 and in 1965,[30] Ian Smith felt sufficiently confident to pursue a unilateral declaration of independence. He countered the British NIBMAR Principles with five of his own: (1) Rhodesia is unable to accept the principle of unimpeded progress toward majority rule enshrined in the 1961 constitution; (2) Rhodesia rejects the idea of any constitutional safeguard that would prevent Europeans in Rhodesia from changing the constitution to prohibit the "premature" emergence of an African government; (3) Rhodesia sees the extension of adult suffrage on the B roll as the only measure of African advancement; (4) Rhodesia intends to take no specific steps toward ending racial discrimination or amending the Land Apportionment Act; (5) Rhodesia will tolerate no procedure of consulting African opinion in Rhodesia which might lead to the rejection of the negotiated agreements between the two governments.[31] The lines were squarely drawn.

[30] In the 1965 Rhodesian general election, out of a total of 68,384 votes cast, the results were as follows: Constituencies: Rhodesian Front, 28,175 (A roll), 206 (B roll); Rhodesia Party, 6,381 (A roll), 505 (B roll); independents, 964 (A roll), 4 (B roll). Electoral districts: Rhodesia Party, 12,936 (A roll), 754 (B roll); independents, 17,770 (A roll), 689 (B roll).

[31] Great Britain Cmnd. 2807 (1965), *Southern Rhodesia: Documents Relating to Negotiations between the United Kingdom and the Southern Rhodesian Governments.*

*The Unilateral Declaration of Independence (UDI)*

At this point, then, a checkmate existed between Britain and Rhodesia. Smith was faced with an articulate white population demanding a declaration. Indeed, his own position as prime minister was dependent on independence being declared. Furthermore, since 1961 there had been more emigration than immigration and capital investments had been declining; he felt that only independence would reverse this trend. The Rhodesian Front went to the country with a referendum on the issue and received 41,949 "yes" votes for a UDI as against 21,846 "no" votes. On November 11, 1965, Rhodesia, therefore, unilaterally declared itself independent.[32]

Britain's immediate response to the UDI was to pass an act declaring the Rhodesian actions void and to ask the Commonwealth to help suppress the revolution. In addition, the foreign secretary, Michael Stewart, flew to New York on November 12 (the day after UDI) and addressed a special meeting of the United Nations Security Council. He said that his government was opposed to any settlement by military force but asked for universal support for measures designed to end the Smith regime and establish lawful government in its place. Immediate measures to be taken included the cessation of all British aid to Rhodesia, an end to the export of arms and munitions, restrictions

[32] The 1965 constitution, promulgated after UDI, was basically the same as the 1961 constitution. Among the changes included in the new document were: (1) the country was named "Rhodesia" instead of "Southern Rhodesia"; (2) the title of the head of state was changed to "The Officer Administering the Government"; and (3) appeals were removed to the Judicial Committee of the Privy Council.

on the purchase of Rhodesian tobacco, and exclusion of Rhodesia from the sterling monetary area. Britain asked members of the United Nations not to accord recognition to the illegal Smith government and also to adhere strictly to similar economic sanctions.[33]

The immediate effect of sanctions on Rhodesia was hard to gauge. The lack of oil caused by the oil embargo, financial difficulties as a result of foreign exchange embargoes, restrictions on imports, and travel difficulties for Rhodesian citizens were obvious inconveniences. Tobacco was, perhaps, the hardest hit. In 1965 the tobacco crop was a record 244,000,000 pounds, but in 1967 it was officially limited to 132,000,000 pounds, and by then the government had a stockpile of 200,000,000 pounds and was limiting the price paid per pound. The government was also subsidizing a diversification plan in which it reduced the number of tobacco growers from 2,700 to 1,800. This diversification adversely affected the balance within the agricultural sector and resulted in an overproduction of maize and, hence, government subsidizing of this sphere of agriculture as well. Potentially more dangerous was the

[33] The Security Council has adopted several resolutions on Rhodesia. It has condemned UDI and called on states not to recognize the illegal Smith regime (Nov. 12, 1965); required all member states to impose selective economic sanctions (Dec. 16, 1966); extended those sanctions to prohibit virtually all trade with, investments in, or transfer of funds to Rhodesia and imposed restrictions on air transport to the territory (May 29, 1968); reaffirmed existing sanctions and required all member states to end consular representation and to interrupt immediately any existing means of transportation to and from Rhodesia (March 18, 1970); expressed concern at violations of sanction provisions and called upon member states to carry out scrupulously their obligation to implement Security Council resolutions (July 28, 1972).

fact that 73,000 fewer African farm workers were employed in 1967 than in 1966. Admittedly, many of these farm workers were from Malawi and Zambia, but, at the same time, only 18,000 new jobs were created in other sectors of the economy for an African labor force growing at the rate of 45,000 persons a year. On the whole, however, the economy remained basically sound (in 1968, there was an 8.6 per cent rise in the G. N. P.), and in some ways it even expanded because of the need for self-sufficiency.[34]

British policy toward Rhodesia was based on two misjudgments: that there would be significant internal opposition among both Africans and whites toward the Rhodesian Front Party and a UDI; and that sanctions would ultimately force white Rhodesians to accept British terms for independence.

[34] In addition there was considerable diversification of secondary industries, particularly those concerned with the production of textiles, footwear, and various forms of machinery.

CHAPTER 2

# Efforts to Resolve the Constitutional Impasse

In its efforts to resolve the constitutional crisis over Rhodesia's Unilateral Declaration of Independence, Britain attempted to have the best of both worlds; while engaging in negotiations, it also imposed a policy of sanctions. The British government operated from outside of the Rhodesian political system but nonetheless played a vital role in the viability and continuation of that system. It had various options open to it, ranging from the use of military force in order to annihilate the rebel regime [1] to total compliance with the *de facto* control of the country by the Smith government. There were also various conflicting factors to be considered—British economic vested interests, the kith and kin argument (i.e., white Rhodesian family ties in Great Britain), African political rights, international pressures, and the active concern of Britain's former African colonies. In the face of these factors, Britain committed itself to a constitutional political solution. However, it aimed at goals that were possibly mutually exclusive: the extension of political rights to Africans and a substantially undiminished white power base. There was some variation between the Labour and Conservative

[1] It is doubtful, however, that the British government would have engaged in the major logistical effort of moving a military force to Rhodesia.

governments in Britain: the Conservatives were at all times more flexible and ready to compromise. On both, however, there were constraints such as the dogged intransigence of Smith and the Rhodesian Front Party, African counterpressures, and the possibility of international vigilance.

Between May and August of 1966, there were three rounds of talks between representatives of the Smith regime and the Commonwealth Relations Office. From December 2 to December 4, 1966, Smith and Wilson met abroad H.M.S *Tiger,* and Harold Wilson made greater concessions than ever before in offering Smith political control—presumably far beyond any mandate from his own Labour Party. As a result of the discussions, a draft proposal emerged under which Rhodesia would agree to suspend temporarily its Declaration of Independence while new constitutional changes were submitted to the Rhodesian people. Although Smith and Wilson arrived at a working document,[2] Smith's mandate was even more limited than Wilson's, and the proposals, once referred back to Salisbury, were rejected. Smith was dependent on a vertically organized party closely in tune with its grass-

[2] The terms of the working document prepared on H.M.S. *Tiger* included the following changes to the 1961 constitution in order to meet at least some of the NIBMAR Principles. The Legislative Assembly was to consist of thirty-three A-roll seats, seventeen B-roll seats, and seventeen Reserved European seats; each block of seats was to cover the whole of Rhodesia. There was to be a Senate consisting of twelve European seats, elected by Europeans on the A roll, six members representing Matabeleland, six members representing Mashonaland, and six chiefs elected by the National Council of Chiefs. As far as the franchise was concerned, the B roll was to include all Africans over the age of thirty who fulfilled the qualifications of residency and citizenship.

roots support.[3] Essentially, Wilson had offered independence for Rhodesia, with Ian Smith, as prime minister, running the country more or less along the lines of the 1961 constitution—thus moving away from NIBMAR. But white Rhodesian Front supporters found this unacceptable and, hence, so did Ian Smith.

The gist of the opposition to the settlement was based on the constitutional ramifications of the agreement and the specific mechanics surrounding its implementation.[4] The Rhodesian government feared that it would be forced to make substantial concessions. Under the terms of the document, Parliament was to be dismissed for four months. Opponents feared that the period of interim government might be extended indefinitely. Furthermore, they pointed out that the White Paper gave no guarantee that as head of the interim government Ian Smith would have any say in the choice of cabinet ministers—the proposals gave the governor wide discretion over the appointment of the members of the interim government. They felt that the governor was there to carry out the instructions of the Commonwealth Relations Secretary rather than to act on the advice of interim ministers. Rhodesian opponents went on to say that the governor, and the proposed British government representatives on the Defense and Security Council, would be in a position to make all major decisions irrespective of the position of the Rhodesian ministers. Finally, they maintained that while the interim government was in office, the British government might find an excuse to send in British military assistance, and that there

[3] See *Africa Report,* Feb. 1967, p. 6.

[4] In January 1967 a White Paper on the *Tiger* talks was tabled by Ian Smith in the Rhodesian Parliament.

was nothing to stop Britain from legally establishing military bases in Rhodesia.

On purely constitutional grounds, Ian Smith was concerned about a return to a 1961-type constitution. "While the constitution outline is acceptable to us, it would be irresponsible of us to abandon the 1965 constitution, under which we are presently working, before we have assurances, without any shadow of doubt, what your constitutional proposals will secure to us, instead of some possible constitution of an unknown nature or a situation in which a constitution might not eventuate." [5] As a consequence of these reservations the constitutional proposals were not accepted.

Because of the breakdown between the British government and the Rhodesian Front, Ian Smith told Parliament in January 1967 that he had decided to establish an impartial commission to report on a new constitution for Rhodesia. Smith also reiterated the position that when Rhodesia accepted the 1961 constitution it did so on the understanding that if the Federation failed this constitution would be the basis of Rhodesian independence. Rhodesia's Declaration of Independence was therefore, in his opinion, not an illegal one, but the result of a contractual agreement between the Rhodesian and British governments. With somewhat melodramatic finality, Smith considered that the door to negotiations with Britain was "finally slammed and locked. . . . Now the British are out of the way, the time has come for Rhodesians to do the job properly ourselves." [6] Harold Wilson went further than ever in offering Smith political control in Rhodesia, and if a settlement had been reached, he would have faced

[5] *Rhodesia Herald,* Jan. 26, 1967. [6] *Ibid.,* Jan. 28, 1967.

internal dissension within his own Labour Party. Furthermore, Smith gave the impression at the *Tiger* talks that he had the authority to come to a settlement on board ship when in fact he did not.[7]

In a response to the breakdown of negotiations with Britain, the congress of the Rhodesian Front Party, in April 1967, decided to delete any reference to the Queen in the party principles and substitute a loyalty oath to the "independent country of Rhodesia." [8] Smith said that he would resist premature pressure for a republic, but that sooner or later Rhodesia would have to face up to the question of becoming a republic.

Even though the Rhodesian public stance acknowledged a growing gap with the British government, it was still willing to negotiate with Britain on the constitutional issue. In June 1967, Lord Alport, former United Kingdom high commissioner to the Federation, visited Rhodesia to see if Ian Smith wanted to resume talks aimed at a settlement, and furthermore to find out whether Smith had the full support of his party. While in Rhodesia, Alport also had meetings with Sir Humphrey Gibbs (whom Britain still recognized as governor of Rhodesia) and African representatives. Commonwealth Secretary George Thomson visited Rhodesia in early November. On his return to Britain, Thomson stated that the changes requested by Smith fundamentally altered the nature of the *Tiger* proposals and that he was not hopeful of an early settlement. Nevertheless, the door should be left open.[9] Several important British politicians visited Rhodesia in the early part of 1968 on unofficial visits. In February, Sir Alec

[7] *Africa Report,* Feb. 1967.
[8] *Rhodesia Herald,* April 24, 1967.
[9] *Ibid.,* Nov. 15, 1967.

Douglas-Home met with Smith and several other Rhodesians. In September, James Bottomley, assistant undersecretary at the Commonwealth Office, met with Ian Smith and Sir Humphrey Gibbs.

In the same month the appellate division of the Rhodesian High Court came to an important decision affecting the question of constitutional settlement when it ruled that the incumbent Rhodesian government had achieved *de jure* status and that the 1965 constitution had to be upheld. The decision was reached unanimously by Chief Justice Hugh Beadle, Judge President Sir Vincent Quenet, and Justice H. N. MacDonald.[10]

## *The* Fearless *Talks*

The comings and goings of British officials led to an announcement by the British government on October 8, 1968, that Harold Wilson and the Rhodesian prime minister would meet on the following day for talks aimed at finding an acceptable settlement for both sides. Rhodesia participated because of its increasing isolation from the world community and its severe balance-of-payments crisis. The talks were to take place on board H.M.S. *Fearless,* which was anchored in Gibraltar harbor. Before attending the meeting, Harold Wilson stated the main questions to be dealt with: guarantees of the first and second NIBMAR Principles; an examination of the braking mechanism that Ian Smith wanted in order to hold back the African involvement in the political process; and the return to constitutional government. When questioned on the access of Africans to the talks, Harold Wilson maintained that he,

[10] *Ibid.,* Sept. 14, 1968.

together with the commonwealth secretary and attorney general, "in addition to representing Britain [would] be representing the 4 million Rhodesian Africans in these discussions." [11] After four days of talks, it was announced that the meetings had ended without an agreement on fundamental issues.[12] However, Ian Smith agreed to put the proposals suggested by Harold Wilson before his cabinet.

The terms of the possible agreement appeared in a White Paper presented to the British Parliament. Wilson said that the six principles were not negotiable and that the *Tiger* proposals were to be closely followed with one major difference concerning the return to constitutional government. A royal commission was to be established to test whether the new independence constitution was acceptable to all Rhodesians.[13] The aim of the British government was simply to ensure African political participation and to guarantee that white Rhodesians did not fundamentally change the character of this participation after a settlement. The Rhodesians, however, were to prove intransigent on the question of political concessions to Africans. Wilson emphasized that there was at all times to be a "blocking quarter" of directly and popularly elected Africans as a safeguard against retrogressive amendment to the constitution. He also stressed the British government's insistence on a program of African education (aimed at increasing the number of African voters) and said that he was prepared to contribute toward this end a sum of £50 million over ten years which should be matched by the Rhodesian government. If the royal commission found the

[11] *Ibid.,* Oct. 10, 1968. [12] *Ibid.,* Oct. 15, 1968.
[13] *Africa Report,* Dec. 1968.

settlement acceptable, the British government would legislate to introduce a Rhodesian independence constitution.

On October 16, 1968, Ian Smith, speaking on radio and television, made a statement on the significance of appeals on entrenched clauses to the Judicial Committee of the Privy Council.[14] "Let me emphasize that my complaint is not against the blocking quarter, but that the British Government wishes to assume additional powers which are a derogation from the sovereignty of our Rhodesian Parliament." [15]

On October 23, Wilson told the House of Commons that he was willing to consider "alternative instruments" for the Judicial Committee of the Privy Council, for example, a judicial committee of Britain, Rhodesia, Australia, New Zealand, South Africa, Malawi, or other African countries, as a possible alternative to such a tribunal. Wilson also suggested that he might be prepared to dispense with the Judicial Committee if he received an understanding that there would be no amendments to entrenched clauses for a given period, say fifteen years.[16]

George Thomson returned to Britain and reported to Parliament that a constitutional safeguard based on a referendum of Rhodesian voters was offered to Ian Smith. It was proposed as an alternative to an appeal to the Privy Council in place of the "second block" guarantee against retrogressive amendments to a Rhodesian independence constitution.

On November 19, 1968, Smith rejected the British posi-

[14] Final appeals rested, not with the Rhodesian High Court, but with the Privy Council in Great Britain. Rhodesia saw this as a limitation of its independence.

[15] *Rhodesia Herald,* Oct. 17, 1968.

[16] *Ibid.,* Oct. 24, 1968.

tion:[17] "under no circumstances can we accept a second-class independence, a constitution that will mean in the end that we are not masters of our own house."[18] It is ironic to note that on November 11, 1968, three years after the Unilateral Declaration of Independence, the Union Jack had been lowered for the last time and a new Rhodesian flag was raised.

### *The Whaley Constitution*

Faced with yet another breakdown in negotiations with Britain, the Rhodesian government once again attempted to resolve the constitutional crisis internally. They were seeking local solutions to what were perceived as purely local problems and were also attempting to establish a *modus operandi* for the country in the absence of an international settlement. In February 1967 a five-man Constitutional Commission was established under the chairmanship of William Whaley[19] in order "to advise the government of Rhodesia on the Constitutional framework which is best suited to the sovereign independent status of Rhodesia . . . and which is calculated to protect and guarantee the rights and freedoms of all persons and communities in Rhodesia and insure the harmonious development of Rhodesia's plural society, having regard to the social and cultural differences among the peoples of Rhodesia, to the

[17] The Rhodesians also wanted to extend the period defined under the 1961 constitution for which the legislature could approve the proclamation of a state of emergency (and hence the time for which Rhodesian citizens could be held in detention without charge or trial) from three to six months.

[18] *Africa Research Bulletin,* Nov. 1–31, 1968.

[19] It also consisted of Charles Mzingeli, the former African trade union leader, Chief Botha Sigola, R. H. Cole, and S. E. Morris.

different systems of land tenure, and to the problems of economic development." [20]

The conclusions of the Whaley Commission in 1968 came as quite a shock to white Rhodesians. Although the commission by no means proposed "one man–one vote," they advocated eventual ("not measured by clock or calendar") [21] political "parity" between black and white in a bicameral legislature. "Europeans must surrender any belief in permanent European domination." [22]

*The Financial Times* commented that the Whaley proposal was essentially one which "would leave effective political power in European hands for all time." [23] None-

[20] *Report of the Constitutional Commission* (Salisbury: Government Printer, 1968). Under its proposals, forty of the lower house's eighty seats would be reserved for white voters, twenty of the remaining would be filled under a qualified roll (£900 income or ownership of property valued at £3,000, or annual income of £600 plus four years of secondary education, or chiefs who were qualified *ex officio*). The twenty other seats would be distributed as follows: twelve for Tribal Trust Lands, six for urban Africans, and two for African purchase areas. The proposals envisaged five voters rolls, a common roll, a special European roll, and three special African rolls —for members of electoral colleges for electing tribal representatives, for African urban areas, and for African purchase areas.

The Senate was to consist of thirty-one members: six chiefs elected by the provincial assemblies of chiefs; six elected African members chosen by tribal and urban electoral colleges; twelve elected European members chosen by an electoral college based on fields of interest; and seven members appointed by the head of state. The number of senators in the first three groups was to be equally divided between Mashonaland and Matabeleland. There was a qualified protection of human rights and amendments to specially entrenched provisions requiring a two-thirds majority in the Legislative Assembly and the Senate, sitting separately, and a three-fourths majority in joint sitting of the Legislative Assembly and the Senate.

[21] *Ibid.* [22] *Africa Report,* June 1968.

[23] *Financial Times* (London), July 1, 1969.

theless, it failed to gain approval from white Rhodesians because of its implications of ultimate African equality. Parity for whites was clearly not enough.

## *The 1969 Constitution*

By the time the special congress of the Rhodesian Front met, from September 5 to 7, 1968, Ian Smith had already received clear inputs on the unacceptability of the constitutional proposal from some members of his cabinet (such as Lord Graham and William Harper), from the party caucus, and from the grass roots. It was not surprising, then, that Smith proposed an alternative measure.

In February 1969, Ian Smith stated that government constitutional experts had been busy for the previous six months drafting a new constitution. He said that a new idea was to be introduced to replace the controversial two-stage parity scheme of the Whaley Commission and that meetings among the six divisional party chairmen would be called throughout the country to explain the new proposal. Smith said that it was his intention to pass a referendum bill in Parliament in April and that a referendum on a constitution would be held in May.[24]

[24] There was to be a national bicameral parliament, the lower house initially consisting of sixty-six members of whom fifty would be elected by white, Coloured, and Asian voters. The remaining sixteen seats would be African, to be given in the form of "credit" because all Africans contributed less than 1 per cent of the income tax paid in Rhodesia. Eight of the sixteen seats would be tribal, elected by chiefs ("the true leaders of the people") and headmen. The other eight would be elected predominantly by urban Africans. As contributions by Africans (calculated in terms of income tax paid) increased, the sixteen seats could become fifty seats. This could eventually bring about a form of parity, with blacks and whites each having fifty seats and with four constituencies each in Mashonaland

Ian Smith felt that he had "the best of both worlds" because the constitution enshrined two important fundamentals of the Rhodesian Front Party: it entrenched government in the hands of "civilized Rhodesians" for all times, and it meant that "merit" would be the criterion for African political involvement. The Senate was to take over the duties of the constitutional council (which had checked legislation to see whether it was consistent with the declaration of rights) and a new declaration of rights which was not to be enforceable by the courts but rather safeguarded by the Senate.

The preamble to the Bill of Rights emphasized that the right of life "will be extended to permit the use of force where it is reasonably justified in the circumstances, for the purpose of suppressing terrorism." [25] There was a continuation of the exception to the right of personal liberty which included arrests ordered by judicial and quasi-judicial authorities, and which permitted preventive detention and arrests in the interests of public safety. Protection from search and entry was also limited, and the right of a person not to be compelled to give evidence at his trial was omitted. Freedom of expression was "guaranteed," subject to provisions which permitted the regulation of the press and other media. Land was classified as

---

and Matabeleland. All African voters on the A and B rolls at that time would be transferred to a segregated African roll with income, educational, and property qualifications. The Senate was to consist of ten white members elected by the House of Assembly, ten chiefs (five from Matabeleland and five from Mashonaland) elected by the Council of Chiefs, and three persons of any race appointed by the head of state.

[25] C.S.R. 32-1969, *Rhodesia, Proposal for a New Constitution,* ch. 5.

European area (44,900,000 acres), African area (45,200,000 acres), and national land (6,400,000 acres). The European area, which included all major cities, was defined as that "in which European interests are paramount." [26]

The key to African political participation under the constitution was an increase in the amount of income tax paid. This was dependent upon two factors: the number of educational facilities available and the earning power of Africans. If the Rhodesian government wanted to make a forward thrust in African education it could have easily done so, but this was a country whose electoral system was geared to educational advancement. In Theo Bull's study, *Rhodesian Perspective,* we read that "the educational qualifications for effective participation in political life are set not according to any reasonable measure of political maturity, but to a judgment of how we can prevent too many Africans from having an effective vote in the foreseeable future." [27]

The disparity between white and African annual income must also be taken into account. The National Convention of Southern Rhodesia of 1960 (which investigated the formulation of the 1961 constitution) reported that wages and salaries were related to living standards, and that there were virtually three such standards in Rhodesia: a white scale, an Asian and Coloured scale, and an African scale.[28] The convention had identified two major obstacles to African advancement: first, the fact that the great majority of semiskilled and unskilled African workers were

[26] *Ibid.,* Part III, chs. 1, 2, 3.

[27] Theodore Bull, ed., *Rhodesian Perspective* (London: Michael Joseph, 1967), p. 83.

[28] H. G. Townsend, *As We Are One* (Gwelo, Rhodesia: Catholic Mission Press, 1962), *passim.*

paid wages well below the poverty datum line, and, second, the acquisition of skills was limited by the prejudices of white employers. It pointed out that "the coexistence of two economies—a relatively modern European market economy and a depressed African subsistence economy—is in the pattern of Rhodesia's race structure." [29]

The new constitution, accepted in a referendum in June 1969 with 54,724 votes in favor and 20,776 against,[30] reinforced a segregated society in which the possibility of majority rule was all but eliminated.[31] The introduction commented: "The Government of Rhodesia believes that the present [1965] constitution is no longer acceptable to the people of Rhodesia because it contains a number of objectionable features, the principal ones being that it provides for eventual African rule and inevitably, the domination of one race by another, and that it does not guarantee that government will be retained in responsible hands." [32] It went on to state that the proposed new constitution would ensure that government remained in responsible hands, would provide Africans with the right to play an increasing part in the government of Rhodesia as they earned it by increased contributions to the national exchequer, and would recognize the right of the African

[29] Kotsho Dube, "The Crisis in Rhodesia," *African Forum,* Winter 1967, p. 44.

[30] *New York Times,* June 22, 1969.

[31] William Harper and Lord Graham, former cabinet ministers politically to the right of Ian Smith, proposed a constitution with separate black and white legislatures: the black legislature was to be limited to local and tribal matters and under the control of the white legislature.

[32] C.S.R. 32-1969, *Rhodesia, Proposals for a New Constitution,* Introduction.

chiefs, as leaders of their people, to take part in the counsels of their nation.

In a radio and television speech at this time Ian Smith declared that the constitution "would reconcile radical differences of race, culture and society . . . and . . . sought to allow development of conditions under which the two main races could live in harmony without fear of dominance or subjugation." It was a means of maintaining "stable and progressive government." [33] The British government's response to the constitution, however, was summed up by Harold Wilson's comment that the Rhodesian plan was a "complete and flat denial" of at least five of Britain's six NIBMAR Principles.

On March 1, 1970, Rhodesia declared itself a republic, claiming to end its "80 year link with the British Crown." [34]

[33] Quoted in *Rhodesian Commentary,* June, 1969.

[34] "Rhodesia Becomes a Republic," *Rhodesian Commentary,* March 1970.

CHAPTER 3

# The Pearce Commission: Catalyst

The presence of the Pearce Commission in Rhodesia in the early part of 1972 not only precipitated significant African political activity but also led to the negation of several widely-held myths actively fostered and adhered to by the Rhodesian Front.[1] Until this point, the RF had taken as axiomatic that most of the African people, in both the rural and urban areas, were relatively quiescent, and that it had their support. It also maintained that the chiefs were the legitimate representatives of the African people, and that the chiefs were in turn loyal to them. Furthermore, within Rhodesia, it considered that the Nationalists no longer had the support of the African people. These assumptions proved to be little more than a façade.

African distrust and suspicion erupted into political activity because of the impending reality of a settlement. Without understanding the specific terms of the settlement, many Africans grasped the fundamental reality that a "yes" vote would lead to the indefinite entrenchment of the Smith regime and the end to Britain's intervention as an active agent in Rhodesian politics. The African National Council responded to these concerns and, with a

[1] "In the long history of dissolution of the Empire, there is no real precedent for the Pearce Commission. The normal British practice has been to negotiate independence with various political leaders of the countries concerned and leave it at that." *Times* (London), Feb. 2, 1972.

rudimentary organization and network, mobilized the large number of Africans who opposed the settlement.

If the RF was out of touch with the extent of African discontent, so too was the British government, which all but excluded Africans in the early discussions leading to the presence of the commission in Rhodesia. Britain was anxious to settle the Rhodesian question and anticipated little opposition, even though it was moving away from the principle of unimpeded progress to majority rule. Perhaps Britain was unaware of prevailing Rhodesian attitudes because over the years it had negotiated primarily with the white power structure and had grown out of touch with genuine African sentiments. But why did the RF agree to testing the proposed settlement in Rhodesia by the commission?

In spite of the fact that Rhodesia had survived six years of unilateral independence, by the end of 1971 it was suffering from a shortage of skilled labor, declining export markets, and a dearth of foreign exchange. In addition, the presence of a Conservative government in Great Britain meant that the Rhodesian government was more willing to reopen negotiations with a special emissary sent by Britain to Salisbury, Lord Goodman. In September 1971, Lord Goodman made the last of several visits to the Rhodesian capital, and throughout October and November rumors of a settlement proposal were widespread. Finally, in November, Sir Alec Douglas-Home, accompanied by a team of advisers, arrived in Salisbury. Referring to the talks, Rhodesian Prime Minister Ian Smith said, "We have made some significant progress.[2] However,

[2] A measure (the Byrd Amendment) to resume the importation of chrome (regarded by the United States as a strategic mineral despite

I have said before, this is no cause for any great optimism, for I would remind you that whenever we met on previous occasions we also made progress—regrettably what proved in the end to be insufficient progress." [3]

The main points of the agreement worked out by Lord Goodman and ratified by Sir Alec Douglas-Home included, on paper, electoral arrangements which would eventually produce an African parliamentary majority. Rhodesia had to declare its intention to make progress toward ending racial discrimination; accept a new declaration guaranteeing individual rights and freedoms; include steps to enable more Africans to compete on equal terms with whites for civil-service jobs; review the cases of all detainees and restricted persons; and set up an independent committee to study racial discrimination and make recommendations to the Rhodesian government. Up to £50 million in British aid was to be given to Rhodesia over a ten-year period, and the Rhodesian government was to match this sum to promote educational and job opportunities for Africans.[4]

The settlement proposal, especially in the fields of agriculture and education, offered Africans, again on paper,

---

a stockpile of 1.3 million tons) was approved in the U.S. Senate and later in the House of Representatives in 1971. The United States thus broke the sanctions imposed by the U.N. Security Council in 1965, albeit on a limited basis, thereby giving the Rhodesian government the right to claim a breakthrough in sanctions at a strategic time in negotiations with Britain.

[3] *Star* (Johannesburg), Nov. 13, 1971.

[4] In 1972 the number of African children receiving some sort of education was 670,451 and the number of white children was 57,000. In form four, the freshman year of high school, 3,090 Africans and 4,441 whites; in upper and lower sixth form, the last two years of high school, 509 Africans and 1,512 whites.

more jobs in the civil service, and it placed restraints on the government's future use of preventive detention, but it left the government with a formidable armory of existing legislation. Britain hoped that such a settlement would hold Rhodesia back from an apartheid position, and, by increasing African participation, albeit on a limited scale, a way might be opened to a more meaningful constitutional involvement in the political process for Africans.

The proposals provided a complicated formula for a gradual increase in African political involvement and opened the way for a possible African government at some distant future date. A new African higher roll was proposed with the same income, property, and educational qualifications for whites and Africans. As the number of Africans on this roll increased, new African seats were to be added in Parliament. When the number of voters registered equalled 6 per cent of the total number of voters registered on the European roll, two African seats would be added; when the number of voters registered equalled 12 per cent, two more seats would be added. Thus, African seats would be added two at a time for each proportionate African increase of 6 per cent. African seats thus created would eventually result in parity in the number of African and white seats in the House of Assembly; the two-by-two increase would continue until there were fifty African seats.[5] At parity, a committee would be appointed to decide how to bring about an African majority government, and their suggestions would require approval by two-thirds of Parliament (essentially giving whites a veto power).

[5] At implementation of the settlement proposals, there were to have been sixteen African members of the House and fifty white members.

The first two additional African seats were to be filled by direct election for single-member constituencies by the voters registered on the African higher roll and the next two by indirect election by electoral colleges, i.e., the chiefs (on the same basis as the existing eight African seats by indirect election). This sequence would be repeated to fill subsequent additional African seats.

The registrar general of voters was to review the number of voters registered on the African higher roll and the European roll at intervals not exceeding six months. The qualifications for the existing roll of African voters (the African lower roll) were to be replaced by qualifications equivalent to those for the B roll under the 1961 constitution, except that the financial qualifications were to be increased by 10 per cent.

Most importantly, a committee was to be appointed by Britain to assess the views of all racial groups in Rhodesia on the acceptability of the settlement proposals.

Britain was clearly anxious to get out of a situation where it had responsibility without power, and hence it was not surprising that it was shifting away from the first of the five NIBMAR Principles, that of unimpeded progress to majority rule, as a condition for recognition of Rhodesia's independence. The purpose of the Pearce Commission was to satisfy the fifth of the principles (to ensure that a settlement would be acceptable to the Rhodesian people as a whole). Under the proposals Britain hoped that at least the economic position, and specifically the standard of living, of Rhodesian Africans would improve.

Analysis of the terms of the settlement indicated a considerable willingness on Great Britain's part to compromise. The proposed terms were far from the guarantees of the relatively liberal 1961 constitution, which permitted whites and blacks to register on a common roll under the same financial and educational qualifications and which promised eventual majority rule. Indeed, the acceptable formula left the white government with considerable influence over African representatives, particularly since two of every four African seats were to go to chiefs.

In 1968, Harold Wilson's Labour government had imposed the requirement that a British judicial council should supervise constitutional issues. Under the 1971 proposals Britain seemed quite willing to accept a declaration of rights with appeals to the courts. While this in itself was something of a milestone (under the 1969 constitution the Declaration of Rights was guaranteed by the Senate and hence open to political tampering), it was by no means a sufficient guarantee.

The major concession Ian Smith made was to abandon his public commitment that Africans would never achieve more than parity in representation in Parliament and to allow at least some African voters to be registered on a common voters' roll with whites at some distant time. Nonetheless, the agreement left whites firmly in control of the advancement of blacks. On the crucial point of racially discriminatory legislation enacted during the previous six years, Sir Alec Douglas-Home appeared to have gained little.

On December 1, 1971, the British House of Commons approved the government's plan for a settlement in Rhodesia by a vote of 297 to 269. Sir Alec Douglas-Home told the House that "in conscience" he did not believe "better terms could have been negotiated" because he felt that

"Britain's influence was running out." He also emphasized that the terms were only in the form of a proposal, and that all now depended on the findings of the commission formed to test opinion on the plan.

The commission was headed by Lord Pearce, a distinguished British judge who had been involved in a number of important royal commissions[6] but who, interestingly enough, had not had any prior African experience. Originally the commission was to have had fifteen members, but by January 1972 the membership had increased to twenty-one. Of the four deputy chairmen, three had had significant experience in Africa. Sir Maurice Dorman had been a former governor of Sierra Leone, Sir Glyn Jones had been a former governor of Malawi, and Sir Frederick Pedler had been a former deputy of the United Africa Company.[7] The fourth deputy chairman was Lord Harlech, who had been British ambassador in Washington. While all of the other commissioners were former colonial officials with extensive service particularly in West and East Africa, there were no African representatives on the commission.[8]

[6] Lord Pearce had been chairman of the Committee of Shipbuilding Costs in 1947, of the Royal Commission of Marriage and Divorce in 1951, and of the Appeals Committee of the Takeover Panel of the City (London's business district).

[7] Pedler withdrew from the commission in January 1972.

[8] Other commissioners appointed were Thomas Cashmore, former district officer in Kenya; Arthur Dawkins, a former district commissioner and provincial commissioner in Sierra Leone; F. W. Essex, a former deputy financial secretary in Sierra Leone and permanent secretary in Swaziland; D. F. H. Frost, a former United Nations specialist adviser to the Swaziland government; J. L. S. Harrison, formerly with the overseas service in Swaziland; Freda Gwilliam, former educational adviser to the colonial office and the ministry of overseas development, who since 1970 had been chairman of the

During the commission's visit all Rhodesians were supposed to have free access to the commissioners in order to discuss the acceptability of proposals. The members of the commission were to be free to travel throughout the country, including the rural African areas, and people in detention or under restriction were to have free access to them.

Before and during the test of acceptability, the commission insisted that normal political activities would be permitted, although it never specified by whom or how this was to be ensured. In her recent book, *The Right to Say No,* Judith Todd indicated that despite the White Paper's promise of normal political activity, J. B. Hove, an African member of Parliament, was not permitted to speak at a meeting by the Belingwe district commissioner, I. C. Bissett, because Bissett had not been given seven days' notice of Hove's intention to speak. She also maintained

executive of Voluntary Service Overseas; Denis Blain, a member of the diplomatic service since 1967; Geoffrey Blake, who spent fifteen years in the Sierra Leone administrative service; John Blunden, district commissioner in a number of centers in Northern Rhodesia; J. H. Burges, a former district commissioner in Northern Rhodesia; Philip Burkinshaw, a former deputy administrator of the Turks and Caicos Islands; John Hayley, who served in Nigeria, Northern Rhodesia, and Bechuanaland; Philip Large, who held several senior posts in the provincial administration in Northern Rhodesia; John Massingham, a member of the diplomatic service and former deputy high commissioner in Sierra Leone; Mark Patey, who served in Swaziland; Colin Rawlins, who served twenty years in Northern Rhodesia; I. E. Butler, who spent thirteen years in the overseas civil service in the Gilbert and Ellice Islands and Swaziland; J. C. Strong, who served as a district commissioner in Tanganyika; A. St. John Sugg, a former provincial commissioner in Northern Rhodesia; and A. H. Whitefield, who served as senior district officer in Northern Nigeria. Statistician for the commission was R. M. Allen, who served ten years as a district officer in Northern Rhodesia.

that African members of the police had told the people that it was useless to oppose the terms, and she cited one instance in which plainclothesmen openly warned people that any organizing of meetings to discuss the White Paper would result in arrests.[9] The commission also insisted on freedom for political parties and on immunity for witnesses in regard to evidence given to the commission. Africans frequently preferred to appear in groups, rather than individually, before the commission, because they were unsure about this immunity. George Fortune, professor of African languages at the University College of Rhodesia, was to preside over two boards to choose interpreters, one for Shona and one for Sindebele. The commission also invited Rhodesians living abroad to express their views.

A statement issued by the Rhodesian prime minister's office on December 19, 1971, said that the terms of reference of the Pearce Commission to test Rhodesian opinion were as follows: "To satisfy themselves that the proposals for a settlement as set out in Annex B to Command 4835 [British White Paper] have been fully and properly explained to the population of Rhodesia; to ascertain by direct contact with all sections of the population whether the people of Rhodesia as a whole regard these proposals as acceptable as a basis for independence; and to report to the Foreign and Commonwealth Secretary accordingly." [10]

Lord Pearce made plain his concern that the people of Rhodesia as a whole understand and accept the terms of

[9] Judith Todd, *The Right to Say No* (Stanford, Calif.: Third Press, 1973), pp. 69, 83.

[10] Quoted in Great Britain Cmnd. 4964 (1972), *Rhodesia: Report of the Commission on Rhodesian Opinion under the Chairmanship of the Right Honourable Lord Pearce,* p. 2.

agreement of the settlement proposals. In a final broadcast before his departure from Rhodesia on March 11, 1972, he said that he hoped there would be no lingering doubts about the independence of his commission. "Our analysis," he said, "will be entirely impartial."[11] It is to the commission's credit that it resisted efforts by the RF to arrange the logistical details of the visit, such as the areas to be visited, who were to be the official translators (the suggestion was that government interpreters would be best), and so on.

Meetings began to take place in Rhodesia on January 17, 1972, and were scheduled to continue for at least two months. No sooner had the commission started work than it became apparent that the proposed settlement was coming under unexpected pressure from spontaneous African opposition to the terms of the agreement. The presence of the Pearce Commission, and the British insistence that the state of emergency be lifted so that there might be a return to African political activity, clearly enabled latent African discontent to emerge.

The operation of the Pearce Commission, in its own words, "opened against a background of mounting tension."[12] On January 16, 1972, large numbers of Africans in the Gwelo area attempted to march to the High Court, where they thought two of the commissioners were holding hearings, in order to inform them of their rejection of the settlement proposals. Several people were killed in a confrontation between the police and the demonstrators. It should be emphasized at this point that this was a particularly tense situation—one in which the arbitrari-

[11] *Rhodesia Herald,* March 11, 1972.
[12] *Pearce Commission,* p. 12.

ness of police provocation cannot be overlooked as a significant contributory factor. In a belated response to widespread, unexpected African opposition, the commissioners at Gwelo postponed the meeting scheduled for that day but continued to work on the following day in an adjacent rural area. When other commissioners met in Fort Victoria, they too found "the atmosphere tense," and disturbances accompanied their visit. On January 19, in Harare, four people were killed in urban rioting. On the same day, in the African township of Umtali, a large crowd was unaware of the postponement of a meeting with the commissioners; when told by the police that there was to be no meeting they broke up into little groups, and eight Africans were killed in the ensuing conflict with the local police.

On January 18, the former Southern Rhodesian prime minister, Garfield Todd, his daughter, Judith Todd, and Ruth and Josiah Chinamano were arrested under section 16 of the Law and Order (Maintenance) Act. The Rhodesian government informed the Pearce Commission that these persons were placed under preventive detention for reasons of internal security. According to Mrs. Grace Todd, six policemen arrived at the family's ranch near Shabani, 300 miles south of Salisbury, to serve the order. It said, "The making of this order is based on the belief that you are likely to commit or to incite the commission of acts in Rhodesia which would endanger the public safety or disturb or interfere with the maintenance of public order." [13]

[13] *New York Times,* Jan. 19, 1972. For many years Garfield Todd had been one of the few prominent whites to act as a bridge be-

In an article headed "Hooligans Do Not Represent African People of Rhodesia" in an official Rhodesian government newspaper, the *African Times,* Ian Smith maintained that "the Government would be failing in its duty if, having negotiated a set of proposals with the British Government which were for the benefit of all Rhodesians —black and white—it permitted a small minority of rabid, militant, nationalist hooligans to jeopardise the test of acceptability now being undertaken by Lord Pearce and his Commissioners." [14] Smith ignored the issue of police provocation and the efforts made by African policemen and district commissioners to intimidate those who organized meetings to discuss the White Paper.

In a belated response to the unexpected African opposition, the ministry of information sent out thousands of pamphlets urging the African people to "say 'Yes' for more schools, 'Yes' for more jobs for Africans, 'Yes' for more African housing, and 'Yes' for better medical facilities." According to the pamphlet, 'yes' meant "development in the Tribal Trust and African Purchase Lands and African political advancement." It concluded, "Tell the Pearce Commission 'Yes,' we Africans accept the proposals. Say 'Yes' for African progress." [15]

The opening debate on the Pearce Commission Report in the Rhodesian House showed that Ian Smith had still not understood the central message of the African discontent. Smith said, "the Africans were deluded into be-

---

tween the Nationalists, the British government, and the Rhodesian public. Because of this, he was regarded with suspicion by the Smith regime.

[14] *African Times,* Feb. 9, 1972.

[15] *Centre Point,* Feb. 1972.

lieving that if they shouted 'no' loudly enough, we would make yet further concessions. I am afraid that they have lost their opportunity." [16] Earlier, Smith had warned the African people that it would be tragic if history recorded that they were so bemused, so susceptible to intimidation, that they rejected an offer which was so much to their advantage. "If the present generation of Africans are so stupid as to reject this offer of advancement for their people," he said, "they will bear the curses of their children forever."

Nevertheless, the Pearce Commission Report released in the last week of May 1972 gave an unequivocal "no" vote to the settlement proposals.[17] Lord Pearce and his commissioners denounced as ill-founded the arguments that either intimidation or ignorance made it impossible for a judgment on the acceptability of the proposals to be formed. The commission said in one of the final paragraphs of the report that it was satisfied that the proposals were fully and properly explained to the people of Rhodesia, and that those who gave an opinion had sufficient understanding of the proposals to enable them to pass judgment. A twenty-six-page dossier presented by the Rhodesian government to the Pearce Commission, however, suggested that there was a definite link between the intimidation and violence and the antisettlement position of the African National Council. Mr. Smith's response to the finding of the commission was that it "had had the wool pulled over

[16] *African Times*, Jan. 26, 1972.

[17] African sentiments regarding the settlement proposals are indicated in the following table from the *Times* (London), May 24, 1972:

its eyes," [18] even though the commission emphasized that it was satisfied after considering all of its evidence, includ-

Public meetings and groups of more than 20

| Area | Acceptances | Rejections | Undecided/ abstaining |
|---|---|---|---|
| Mashonaland North | 50 | 11,600 | 420 |
| Mashonaland South | 30 | 16,500 | 40 |
| Salisbury | 100 | 9,000 | 700 |
| Midlands | 10 | 16,400 | 70 |
| Victoria | 240 | 18,400 | 140 |
| Manicaland | 70 | 18,300 | 70 |
| Matabeleland North | 110 | 2,500 | 180 |
| Matabeleland South | 30 | 5,000 | 200 |
| Bulawayo | 30 | 100 | 10 |
| Totals | 670 | 97,800 | 1,830 |

Groups of less than 20 and individuals

| Area | Acceptances | Rejections | Undecided/ abstaining | Total |
|---|---|---|---|---|
| Mashonaland North | 366 | 853 | 690 | 13,979 |
| Mashonaland South | 245 | 688 | 165 | 17,668 |
| Salisbury | 401 | 2,974 | 287 | 13,462 |
| Midlands | 175 | 1,107 | 151 | 17,913 |
| Victoria | 221 | 579 | 170 | 19,750 |
| Manicaland | 93 | 347 | 67 | 18,947 |
| Matabeleland North | 236 | 467 | 690 | 4,183 |
| Matabeleland South | 226 | 1,205 | 54 | 6,715 |
| Bulawayo | 301 | 1,289 | 187 | 1,917 |
| Totals | 2,264 | 9,509 | 2,461 | 114,534 |

[18] *Star,* May 27, 1972.

ing the intimidation, that the majority of Africans rejected the proposals.

Perhaps the most important result of the African response to the Pearce Commission was that it undermined the fundamental premise of the white government's racial philosophy. The Rhodesian Front had worked hard to restore the powers of the chiefs, whom Ian Smith insisted were the "true leaders" of the African people. The 245 Shona and Matabele chiefs received salaries from, and were supported by the government, and were regarded as the true political spokesmen of the African people.[19] One team of commissioners maintained that "the inescapable conclusion is that the African people, whether rural or urban, do not recognize the chiefs' authority in matters outside tribal custom." [20]

The central reality of the findings of the Pearce Commission is summed up in the following statement: "the *least* requirement for democratic government is that there must exist adequate communication between those who govern and the governed. It is here that the Pearce Commission exposed a fundamental weakness in Rhodesia." [21]

[19] The commission saw 77 per cent of the country's chiefs; 47 per cent rejected the terms, 29 per cent "did not know" or would not give an opinion, 24 per cent said "yes." The commissioner of chiefs had initially urged all Africans to vote yes (*Star,* June 17, 1972).

[20] *Ibid.*

[21] Ken Mew, principal of the Ranche House College, in an address delivered on April 7, 1972 (*Centre Point,* May 1972).

CHAPTER 4

# White Rhodesia: Perspectives and Mechanisms of Control

Margery Perham once remarked that white Rhodesia was a micronation equivalent to a medium-sized British town.[1] How has this micronation, about 80 per cent of whom live in the urban areas, been able to develop and retain control over the African population for so long? A partial answer is to be found in the fact that after the period of early settlement, Rhodesia was a unique case; it was never a formal colonial possession of Great Britain but moved from control by the British South Africa Company to a special, internally self-governing status in which it was administered by the Dominions office.[2] Rhodesia came into being at a time when the British were no longer expanding their colonial empire but were beginning to feel many of the burdens of administering their possessions. This resulted in a greater permissiveness toward Rhodesia than might otherwise have been the case. "Early Rhodesia was almost a monarchy, and Cecil John Rhodes its uncrowned king. In spite of the country's constitutional trappings, the Old Man's word was almost law." [3]

The bypassing of regular procedures became an im-

[1] Margery Perham, "The Rhodesian Crisis: The Background," *International Affairs*, 62, no. 1 (Jan. 1966), p. 4.

[2] For all practical purposes, however, the Rhodesian government was in complete control.

[3] Lewis H. Gann, *A History of Southern Rhodesia: Early Days to 1934* (London: Chatto and Windus, 1965), p. 209.

portant part of Rhodesian constitutional thinking.[4] As a consequence of these factors, the settlers were able to make claims and to exert controls which, although seriously challenged, were never really undermined until 1965.

The heritage in public attitudes of the settlement period has been the notion that the settlers were simply to displace all existing African institutions and culture and erect a modern state in which the African's place was largely undefined. He belonged in the Reserve, and provided a cheap basis of the domestic economy.[5] Apart from this, the African and white communities lived in separate airtight compartments, "so it is impossible to know what the wishes and aspirations of the other sector of the community are." [6] How did the white superstructure come into being, and what is its composition?

The first white settlers were lured by the prospect of a mining Eldorado which did not exist. Few of the early pioneers were specialists; they included soldiers, policemen, civil servants (with a taste for outdoor existence), cattle traders—all with one thing in common: pioneer individualism.[7] When the settlers realized that gold deposits were not widespread, they turned to agriculture, which expanded rapidly after initial difficulties caused by poor communications, limited markets, and the prevailing uncertainties of rural life. Increased agricultural settlement exacerbated tensions between the Africans and the white settlers. The disputes over mineral rights between Loben-

[4] See Robert Rotberg, "Then and Now in Central Africa," *Africa Report,* May 1968.

[5] See Colin Leys, *European Politics in Southern Rhodesia* (Oxford: Clarendon Press, 1959), p. 234.

[6] Chad Chipunza, quoted in *Central African Examiner,* Oct. 1965.

[7] Rotberg, in *Africa Report,* May 1968, p. 163.

gula and Rhodes's agents did not as directly impinge on African landholdings as did the establishment of farms. The combination of settlement, mineral prospecting, and the white political, economic, and religious presence resulted in the hostilities of the Shona and Matabele rebellions, for "there was no other way at the time to eradicate the social and cultural incompatibilities." [8]

The character of white society in Rhodesia today has been shaped by several factors: the settlers' struggle against a hostile environment; their conflict with the indigenous people; their fight for political self-determination; and the fact that African interests were not to be primary in the development of the area. The early conflict situation was replaced by a form of paternalism in which the African was invariably the servant rather than the master, the employee rather than the employer, and so on. Rhodesia could be referred to as a composite society only in economic terms; Africans and whites were jointly engaged (with whites in leadership roles) in mining, farming, the railways, and construction work, but no further. In the early period the primary aim of preserving white supremacy was established, and the only thing that differed over time was the means with which this was to be accomplished. The whites had struggled against the controls of the British South Africa Company to win a measure of self-determination and were reluctant to sacrifice it by joining South Africa. Clear patterns of conflict against authority and of Rhodesia choosing "to go it alone" are also legacies from this period.

[8] Cyril A. Rogers and C. Frantz, *Racial Themes in Southern Rhodesia: The Attitudes and Behavior of the White Population* (New Haven: Yale University Press, 1962), p. 23.

Although Rhodesia decided not to join South Africa in 1923, the importance of South African influences cannot be overestimated. In the settlement period, many Afrikaans farmers came to Rhodesia and settled in areas such as Melsetter, Enkeldoorn, and Chipinga. With an internal solidarity based on their religion, language, and culture, the Afrikaners have remained a unified and important pressure group. Because of their roots in South Africa and also because, on the whole, Afrikaners were on the lower level of the white socioeconomic structure (farming, working in the mines or railways, or building roads) they have strongly opposed policies of African advancement. Thus they backed the Dominion Party against Sir Edgar Whitehead, and were part of the right wing of the Rhodesian Front Party. South Africa had also been an important variable in other ways; a considerable number of the skilled white Rhodesian labor force had come from the south. In addition, from the early 1900's onward, both white and African Rhodesians attended high schools and universities in South Africa. It is interesting to note that according to the 1961 census, only 35 per cent of the white population had been born in Southern Rhodesia; 26.5 per cent were born in South Africa and 26.15 per cent in the United Kingdom.

## *The Franchise as a Mechanism of White Control*[9]

When Southern Rhodesia was granted a form of representative government in 1898, there was no statement con-

[9] Information and statistics on the franchise are compiled from F. M. G. Willson, ed., *Source Book of Parliamentary Elections and Referenda in Southern Rhodesia, 1898–1962* (Salisbury: University College of Rhodesia and Nyasaland, Department of Government, 1963).

cerning the type of franchise to be implemented. The high commissioner in South Africa had the authority to introduce the franchise after consulting the administrator of Southern Rhodesia. Considering Rhodes's involvement in the Cape Parliament, first as a member and then as prime minister, it comes as no surprise that the voting arrangement contained in Proclamation 17 of 1898 was taken from the Cape—the so-called colorblind franchise. Essentially, none of the restrictions introduced was based on color considerations; theoretically, the same qualifications applied to both Africans and whites: they had to be over twenty-one years of age, British subjects (or persons who had taken an oath of allegiance to the Crown), and of sound mind. But in practice the property and education qualifications excluded most Africans. There was a literacy test which required that the person sign his name and write his occupation and address. The property qualifications required residence for the preceding six months in the electoral district and occupation of property valued at not less than £75, or the ownership of a registered mining claim or an annual salary of not less than £50. Communal or tribal occupation of land did not fulfill the requirement.

As early as 1906 qualifications began to be increased in order to exclude the few Africans who were qualified. In 1906 the administration drafted an ordinance which would have prevented more Africans from going on the voters' roll. The measure might well have been put before the legislature, but Lord Selborne, the high commissioner, thought that the secretary of state would veto such a law. Lord Selborne did not object to an alternative suggestion that the property qualification be raised, a measure which would have the additional advantage of keeping poor Afrikaners and semidestitute foreigners with British naturalization certificates out of politics. Considering all of the restrictions, it is remarkable that by 1911 there were fifty-one Africans on the roll. However, many of those who were registered were not local but had emigrated from South Africa.

In 1912 the qualifications were raised again. A potential voter was required to fill out the whole claim form himself and, if asked to do so, to write fifty words of English dictation. The minimum property ownership was raised to £150 and the minimum annual wage to £100.

The 1923 constitution made no basic change in the franchise. In 1928, however, the dictation clause was removed, possibly because of the increase in the number of white immigrants from Europe. The financial restrictions were still sufficient to exclude most Africans.

The franchise remained unchanged until 1951, when the financial arrangements were once again changed; the means requirement was increased to an income of £240 per annum and occupation of property valued at not less than £500. The prospective voter also had to be able to complete and sign the necessary forms and speak and write in English.

In the general election of 1928, 62 African votes were cast out of a total of 21,185. The inequality of the situation had improved little by 1956, when Africans cast 560 votes in the federal referendum, out of an electorate of 49,060.

## *Temporary Deflection from the Norm in Southern Rhodesia*

In 1957, after Southern Rhodesia had been joined in a federation with Northern Rhodesia and Nyasaland, Garfield Todd, who had succeeded Sir Godfrey Huggins as prime minister of Southern Rhodesia, appointed a commission under the chairmanship of Sir Robert Tredgold to re-examine the Southern Rhodesian franchise and to find a means of extending African participation. The commission was "to consider and report on a system for the just representation of the people of the colony in its Legislative Assembly, under which the Government is placed, and remains in the hands of civilized and responsible persons." [10] The Tredgold Commission recommended a common voters' roll; that is, all regular voters, even if they had different qualifications, would vote for the same candidates. The qualifications were based on education, property, and income, and hence, at least on paper, they appeared to go beyond racial restrictions.[11]

The Southern Rhodesian political system had been dominated by whites from 1924 to 1957, with inputs and outputs primarily determined by, and for the interests of, the closed white minority. In terms of party politics, Southern Rhodesia was clearly a one-party system. As

[10] *Report of the Franchise Commission* (Salisbury: Government Printer, 1957), p. 1.

[11] Qualifications included adequate knowledge of English and the completion of the registration form in handwriting; an annual income of at least £720 during the two previous years and possession of real estate worth at least £1500, or income of £480 and real estate worth £100 plus primary education, or income of £300 and real estate valued at £500 plus four years of secondary education. It is of interest to note that the federal qualifications were very similar.

Colin Leys maintains, the changes, splits, and fusions which occurred took place within the framework of the two permanent institutions, the government and the opposition parties; the government party, with the support of the establishment, retained power throughout the period.[12]

Garfield Todd's defection from this norm was more of an individual one than an indication of a significant change in white sentiment. Sir Edgar Whitehead introduced reforms because he was a pragmatic politician attempting to retain an equilibrium for his party in a changing political environment. He was responsible for the restrictive Law and Order (Maintenance) Act, and yet, at the same time, he introduced liberal reforms. Unlike Todd, who tried to change the character of Rhodesian society significantly by extending rights and privileges to Africans, Whitehead introduced changes that were not widely felt because of the inequities of Rhodesian life. They were, rather, pragmatic political responses which he hoped would enable his party to retain power and help Rhodesia to gain independence from Britain. He was aware of the changing context of politics in Africa, and hence began as early as 1959 to de-emphasize the overtly racist elements of Rhodesian legislation—for example, the Industrial Conciliation Act (1934) aimed at removing racial distinctions from labor negotiations and from the settlement of labor disputes. The 1961 constitution for Southern Rhodesia introduced by the United Federal Party was a response to the interdependent goals of amelioration of African discontent and independence from Britain.

The UFP introduced parliamentary changes on two

[12] Leys, *European Politics*, p. 173.

levels: (1) in regard to the franchise and (2) in respect to the composition of the Legislative Assembly. In the 1961 constitution the common roll was replaced by a dual-roll system. Voters with higher qualifications were placed on an A roll, and those with lower qualifications went on a B roll. The qualifications for the A roll were the same as those for the former higher-roll qualification, although chiefs and headmen were now placed on the A roll *ex officio*. The B-roll qualification was to remain in effect indefinitely, not, as with the 1957 reform, to fall away when voters on the lower roll reached a stipulated portion of the electorate.

The opposition Dominion Party, led by William Harper, saw itself as a white party containing the African threat to the existing order. It felt that the future of white civilization depended on the result of the 1961 referendum. Harper was particularly opposed to the presence of African members in the Southern Rhodesian Parliament and the possibility of African cabinet ministers. (Sir Edgar Whitehead had proposed that if he won the election, there would be one African cabinet minister, and by the following election, possibly between three and six such ministers). Harper maintained that "to have Africans in this House at this stage . . . is going to damage the structure of European tenure in this country. Whether one likes it or not, European tenure is sensitive to the fact that the African has not proved his case to take part in the administration of the country as a whole." [13]

Beyond this consideration, Harper voiced the more obvious aspects of Rhodesian intolerance: "I myself can

[13] Southern Rhodesia, *Debates of the Legislative Assembly (Hansard)*, Aug. 23, 1960.

visualize that if we have them in the House they will share the restaurant with us, and they will share the bars with us. We will be living cheek by jowl with them and what sort of legislation can the people of this country expect when we ourselves are being conditioned to living cheek by jowl with Africans." [14] He also played on a theme popular with white Rhodesian extremists: the ineptitude of African leaders in other parts of the continent.

I myself do not feel that we should support the view that some leaders in other parts of Africa are putting forward and which seem to be current. If I may quote one here, and I cannot verify the truth of this, I give it for what it is worth. This is Mr. Oginga Odinga from the Kenya Legislative Council and he is reported to have said, "I think it is for the African people to decide what type of lives they are going to live in their own country. If they decide that savagery is the most fitting thing then they will decide on it." Now I cannot support that point of view that anything goes. I think we have got to stand—we have got to set the standards and we have got to see that they are carried through.[15]

Harper realized that African participation was the key to Southern Rhodesia's independence from Britain, but this was too high a price for the Dominion Party: "I have read what the Prime Minister had to say the other day about having Africans in the House. He wanted everyone to realize how representative the House is of Africans, but that is not an adequate reason, and the only reason one can see at the present moment is that this would induce the United Kingdom Government to feel that Parliament is truly representative of Africans and Europeans, and therefore it must inevitably mean that this is the price this

[14] *Ibid.* [15] *Ibid.,* June 30, 1960.

country is paying for the removal of the restrictions."[16] Sir Edgar Whitehead was able to rally sufficient support to win the constitutional referendum, probably because, as James P. Barber maintains, "from the sheer complexity of the constitutional position, some of the electorate were misled into thinking that they were genuinely voting for independence."[17]

Neither the UFP nor the RF was offering immediate majority rule; in fact, their difference was mainly one of degree. This becomes evident in a more careful examination of the constitution and, in particular, of the Declaration of Rights, which protected, among other things, individual life, liberty, security of the person, enjoyment of property and the protection of the law, freedom of conscience, freedom of expression, freedom of assembly and association, and respect for a citizen's private and family life. Superficially, this statement cannot but appear to be profoundly humanitarian, but, as Kenneth Wheare writes, no realistic attempt to define the rights of the citizen can

[16] *Ibid.,* Aug. 23, 1960.

[17] With the withdrawal of the African Nationalists from constitutional politics, the referendum and the election of 1962 was essentially a struggle between white reactionaries and the "establishment" (James P. Barber, *Rhodesia: The Road to Rebellion* [London: Oxford University Press, 1967], p. 94).

Willson (*Source Book,* p. 187) gives the following statistics for the constitutional referendum of July 26, 1961:

| | | |
|---|---|---|
| Total electorate | 83,486 | |
| Total effective votes | 63,850 | |
| Percentage poll | 76.48 | |
| Rejected papers | 558 | |
| Total in favor of constitution | 42,004 | (65.79%) |
| Total against constitution | 21,846 | (34.21%) |
| Majority in favor of constitution | 20,158 | (31.57%) |

fail to include qualifications. When we see the results it is difficult to resist asking what of the substance is left after the qualifications are given full effect.[18]

An individual was protected by the 1961 constitution against laws that discriminated on the grounds of race, political opinion, and creed as follows: this protection was subject to the rights and freedoms of others and to "the public interest," and it did not apply to laws in force before November 1, 1962.[19] Thus the Land Apportionment Act and the Law and Order (Maintenance) Act were conveniently excluded. The introduction of the latter in 1960 led to the resignation of the federal chief justice, Sir Robert Tredgold, who described it as outraging almost every basic human right and as "an unwarranted invasion" by the executive in the sphere of the courts.[20] "The cumulative effect . . . was to turn Rhodesia into a police state. The word has an emotional content and many white Rhodesians become very angry if it is used of their country. Yet, as I understand it, a 'police state' is a state in which the police and the executive are given or assume political control over all political activity. In this sense it is manifestly true of the Rhodesia of to-day." [21]

Moreover, the Declaration of Rights did not apply to money matters—taxation, government expenditure on education, employment, and so on. Hence there could be discrimination on such matters as participation in

[18] K. C. Wheare, *Modern Constitutions,* 2d ed. (London: Oxford University Press, 1966), p. 52.

[19] Muriel Horrell, *Days of Crisis in Rhodesia* (Johannesburg: South African Institute of Race Relations, 1965), p. 15.

[20] *Times* (London), Nov. 2, 1960.

[21] Robert I. Tredgold, *The Rhodesia that Was My Life* (London: Allen and Unwin, 1968), pp. 230–231.

government, freedom of movement, allocations for African education, and choice of occupation and place of residence. The declaration could be overridden on the grounds of public safety, interest, order, morality, or health. A law dealing with action during a period of public emergency could not be held to be inconsistent with the declaration, nor could lawful orders restricting a person's freedom of movement.

Nonetheless, by 1962 the UFP was beginning to formulate policy that was not supportable by its own members, let alone the Rhodesian electorate. The central issues involved in the election that year were the Land Apportionment Act (which Harper vowed to retain if the Dominion Party won the election), the extension of the Legislative Assembly to include African members, and the whole question of greater African franchise participation. Whitehead felt that African participation would help him to win the election and that the provisions of the constitution would enable Southern Rhodesia to win independence from Britain; he advocated a policy of gradual black-white partnership which he hoped would resolve the constitutional issue. In February 1962, William Harper resigned as leader of the Dominion Party to allow a more cohesive opposition to emerge; by March the Rhodesian Front Party had been formed under the leadership of Winston Field, then a federal M.P. The white electorate began to mass behind this party, "conscious that the real opposition was outside the Legislature and that it was Black. This was the very situation which Sir Edgar had tried unsuccessfully to avoid." [22]

The movement against the UFP had been quite dis-

[22] Horrell, *Days of Crisis,* p. 15.

cernible from about 1958 onward. In 1954 the UFP held twenty-six seats in the Southern Rhodesian Parliament and the opposition held four; in 1958 it held only seventeen seats and the Dominion Party held thirteen. The referendum gave a plurality to the UFP, but the 1962 election (following the implementation of the constitution) returned to the earlier trend: the UFP won only twenty-nine seats (45 per cent of the votes cast—15 A-roll and 14 B-roll seats); the RF won thirty-five seats. Moreover, in the 1965 election the RF won all fifty constituencies and the Rhodesia Party (RP), the UFP's successor, won only the fifteen B-roll electoral district seats.[23] The conservatives had captured all the white electorate.

It has been suggested that had Whitehead's policy of partnership been given a chance it could have avoided what was fast becoming a "simple conflict of race."[24] Garfield Todd saw the decline of the UFP from another perspective: "If there had been a measure of cooperation between the African Nationalist groups and the Whitehead group, Whitehead would have immediately gotten independence for Rhodesia; Whitehead would have been out, the RF would have been in so that the RF would have had the whole power—on the broad basis African nationalists Ndabaningi Sithole and Joshua Nkomo were right in not cooperating."[25]

The 1962 election clearly marks the point of polarization between white exclusionism and black nationalism. From then on there were no half measures. The RF immediately set about counteracting the UFP's "partnership" legislation and consolidating its position. White

[23] Barber, *Rhodesia,* p. 167. [24] Willson, *Source Book, passim.*
[25] Garfield Todd, interview, Salisbury, July 23, 1967.

Rhodesians were now speaking of "disorder," "chaos," and "intimidation"; partnership and cooperation were all but forgotten.

With an unbroken string of political successes behind it, the RF was in a dominant position in Rhodesia. It was well aware that it had the backing of the white electorate and that for most political purposes Rhodesia was a one-party state. Barber has accurately commented that to gauge the sense of participation one should recall that in a population of little more than 200,000 Europeans, about one in five adults is actually enrolled in the party and that each of the fifty RF members of Parliament represents only about 1,500 voters. Anyone who takes an interest in party affairs is sure to know at least his own M.P. and is likely to know others. The fact that Rhodesia's white community is so small makes it easy for all white voices to be heard.[26] And virtually all, explicitly or tacitly, supported continued white control.

The RF based its appeal on two claims. First, it claimed to have saved Rhodesia from black domination by either Joshua Nkomo of the African nationalist organization Zimbabwe African Peoples' Union (ZAPU) or Ndabaningi Sithole, leader of the Zimbabwe African National Union (ZANU). As Sir Roy Welensky pointed out in 1967, this was a completely erroneous idea:

> As far as the European is concerned, you have got to face up to the fact that a magnificent job of brain washing has been done in Rhodesia. Most Rhodesians today firmly believe that in 1966 when Mr. Smith took his independence the choice was a choice between Mr. Nkomo as Prime Minister and Mr. Smith; that the British Government was almost on the point of en-

[26] Barber, *Rhodesia,* p. 17.

forcing some sort of government of which Mr. Nkomo would be the head of Rhodesia. Nothing, of course, was further from the truth.[27]

Second, the RF believed that it was taking a necessary stand against world communism. As Ian Smith himself said in an interview the same year:

Well, I don't think there is any doubt that the root of our trouble—I think that the root of a lot of trouble which we see in the world today is communism—I have said this many times—it is very difficult for us of course to believe that the actions taken by the British Government are completely communist inspired—but I am completely clear in my mind that the forces who are in the main opposed to us and who receive support from the British Government and many other western nations are completely communist. . . . I think we can prove that we are holding the line against the communist infiltration down the African continent. This line, I believe, is at the moment on the Zambezi River.[28]

Patterns of racial interaction established in the settler period had remained unchanged until Sir Edgar Whitehead's efforts to respond to the needs of Rhodesian society as a whole. With the demise of the United Front Party, there was, thus, both a return to, and an elaboration on, the basic white-supremacy norm of the settler period.

The RF itself has had to contend with the continued presence of elements that lay to its own right. The United Front, yet another in a series of right-wing political groups (others had included the Rhodesian Candour League) was established with the overriding principle that "the

[27] Interview, Salisbury, Aug. 24, 1967.

[28] Ian Smith, interviewed by E. Butler (director general, Australian Anti-Communist League), Salisbury, Aug. 10, 1967.

white man's position must be supreme for all time." [29] It advocated "that each community in Rhodesia preserve its own identity, traditions and customs" and saw the need to "provide separate facilities and amenities for the various groups to enable them to preserve their customs and ways of life." [30] The presence of groups like these help to explain why, despite its sensitive constitutional negotiations with Britain, the RF, in order to maintain internal control, increasingly established apartheid-type policies such as legislation which required Africans to carry registration certificates,[31] segregation of facilities, and so on, in order to survive in white Rhodesia.

[29] From statement issued by United Front, *African Research Bulletin,* Feb. 1–29, 1972.

[30] *South African Observer,* 27, no. 2 (April 1972).

[31] *New York Times,* Nov. 18, 1972.

CHAPTER 5

# The Past in the Present: Chiefs in Rhodesia

Chieftainship, currently presented as a bulwark of white control, has undergone several radical transformations over the years. From the early 1900's until the 1920's the whites viewed chieftainship as an institution which had to be subjugated and transformed; the Ndebele and Shona rebellions were resolved by the compliance of the chiefs, based on their realization that the active continuation of the conflict would be futile. The chiefs then became little more than minor bureaucrats or adjuncts to the native commissioners. In contemporary Rhodesia, the anachronistic colonial concept of indirect rule has been revived, and the government regards the chiefs as the legitimate voice for African aspirations. The 1969 Rhodesian constitution established potentially important national political roles for the chiefs in the Senate. On this basis, the Rhodesian Front government maintained that it had provided a legitimate channel for African political activities.

Although chiefs differ in power, influence, and authority, it can be said that Rhodesian chiefs rarely tend to be political or social innovators; that they owe their allegiance to the white power structure which ratifies their appointments and pays their salaries; and that they have alienated large numbers of their traditional supporters.[1] Thus, while

[1] At best, they maintain a precarious balance between these two conflicting interests.

the institution has been actively promoted by the government, it has been frequently rejected by the African people because it represents both the force of the past in a dynamic and changing world and, more importantly, collaboration with the white system.

## *Traditional Shona Political Structure*

The Shona never had a centrally organized state, but rather operated in autonomous political units. Chiefdoms were divided into wards under subchiefs, and these in turn were further divided into small settlements under headmen. In general, Shona chiefs in the nineteenth century did not have a great deal of power, nor was their power widely felt. They had no standing armies, no highly organized structure of political subordinates, and, because the spirit mediums were considered to be in direct contact with the ancestors, little religious authority. Because their power was limited, the chiefs often had to use persuasion in order to gain the voluntary submission of their people. Hilda Kuper maintains: "It was a rare man who chose to wield dictatorially any powers granted by the system. He was usually controlled by bonds of custom and by the knowledge that he had to win and keep the voluntary submission of the people to his authority. If they did not like him, they were at liberty to break away and to sue to join some other group." [2] The considerable instability in the whole system of Shona chieftainship was due primarily to the rules of succession, which tended to produce a number of competing claims for office. After the founder

[2] Hilda Kuper, "The Shona," in *The Shona and Ndebele of Southern Rhodesia,* Hilda Kuper *et al.,* eds. (London: International African Institute, 1954), p. 31.

of a chiefdom died, he was succeeded by all of his sons in turn. When the last died, the eldest son of the founder's first son succeeded, followed by the eldest son of the second, and so on. G. Kingsley Garbett comments: "In the 19th Century, chiefdoms appear to have been proliferating through time. There was a strong tendency on the part of royals who were competing for office, and others, who for one reason or another were disgruntled, to break away and join or form new chiefdoms." [3]

### *The Ndebele Political System*

The Ndebele state stands in sharp contrast to that of the Shona. The Ndebele kingdom was geared for military conquest, and the king was the focal point and the center of all authority. He was the head of the army, owned all cattle and land, and was the final judge of all disputes. The disparate parts of the kingdom were all interconnected; the state was divided into provinces, each under a great chief, and these in turn were divided into regiments with politically controlled towns as their bases. These towns were subdivided under the control of headmen. All within the political structure ultimately owed allegiance to the king and were oriented toward the capital; young warriors received training at Bulawayo, and the king often visited the different towns in which his wives and daughters played strategic synthesizing roles.

### *White Patterns of Control*

Shortly after the Ndebele and Shona rebellions, white patterns of control began to be established over Southern

[3] G. Kingsley Garbett, "The Chief's Dilemma: Government Officer or Tribal Leader" (manuscript, University College of Rhodesia); subsequently published in *Race,* 8, no. 2 (1967), 2.

Rhodesian Africans. In 1893 the Native Affairs Department was established—"a second hierarchy which dealt with African affairs, and soon began to perfect its methods." [4] In 1894 the first two Reserves were created; and in 1895 poll taxes, collected by the native commissioners, were imposed as a coercive device for getting Africans involved in the white economic system. The commissioners also controlled the use of land, served in a magisterial capacity, restricted the use of cattle, and, until 1903, when the Rhodesian Native Labour Bureau was established, acted as such a bureau for the white towns and farming areas. Their position was more complex than the mere administration of Africans: "they acted as magistrates, but they also had to prosecute transgressions of government laws; as administrative officers, they informed the people of government decisions, but they were obliged to see that government intentions were carried out. At the same time, they were responsible for agriculture and animal husbandry, for road work and for all other needs of the districts under their control." [5]

The use of local chiefs to carry out the laws and policies of the white administrators diminished both the authority and the functions of the chiefs. In particular, the white man's power to appoint and depose chiefs and to control the land implied the presence of a superior authority: "the District Commissioner had usurped the secular authority of the chiefs. . . . The realization convinced both the African people and their chiefs that a new era had

[4] Lewis H. Gann, *A History of Southern Rhodesia: Early Days to 1934* (London: Chatto and Windus, 1965), p. 147.

[5] Sister Mary Aquina, O.P., "Modern Chieftanship and the Struggle for Power among the Karanga" (thesis, Manchester University, 1965), p. 17.

begun and that their traditional way of life had gone forever."[6] The chiefs had been replaced by an outwardly efficient and organized bureaucratic structure. The chief native commissioner was at first responsible to the administrator, and later to the Legislative Assembly and the governor.[7] He supervised native commissioners and assistant native commissioners in seven districts. "At the bottom of the administrative pyramid stood the native chiefs who were left with only very limited powers by the law."[8]

The policy of direct rule imposed by the administrators was a conscious and clearly determined one. Because of the rebellions, there was an unwillingness to vest too much power in the chiefs or to strengthen traditional institutions. The policy of direct rule had been implemented successfully in South Africa; and because many of the commissioners came from Natal (because of their experience in working among the Zulu they were considered well qualified), they continued to use a policy which they had tried and found successful.

The new political and administrative organization had a far stronger impact on the Ndebele traditional structure than it did on the Shona. With the exile of the Ndebele king, Lobengula, and the defeat of the regiments and destruction of the towns, the political unity of the kingdom was fragmented. Because of their small, scattered chieftainships, the Shona were not as immediately affected. In

[6] *Ibid.*

[7] The post of chief native commissioner of Rhodesia was established in 1914. Prior to this date there were two, one for Mashonaland and one for Matabeleland. An Order-in-Council of 1898 placed the chief native commissioner under the direct control of the British government.

[8] Gann, *History of Southern Rhodesia,* p. 148.

both instances, however, interference with traditional patterns of authority and migration to the white areas of large numbers of Africans corroded the powers of the chiefs. Some regimental Ndebele chiefs were retained in the new bureaucracy, but no paramount chiefs; on the lower level, headmen were installed at the discretion of the native commissioners. The Shona chiefs were recognized and utilized in a more haphazard fashion; traditional divisions were ignored, and frequently persons with vague claims to a title were recognized because of their willingness to cooperate with the authorities. From the outset, those chiefs who were recognized were paid allowances and subsidies; and hence, the pattern of dependence on the white structure began.

In many ways, the native commissioners sought to reconcile contradictory ends; they wanted to remove the powers of the chiefs, but they did not wish to make them ineffective as agents of the white government. By the 1920's, both the chiefs and the district commissioners were becoming aware that the traditional system was disintegrating. Religious separatist movements, with political overtones, were springing up, and the urban elites were starting to break ties with the rural past. In an effort to counteract these trends, the 1923 constitution provided for the establishment of African councils, and from 1924 onward, meetings took place between the administration and the chiefs and headmen of different districts. In 1931, native boards were established consisting of chiefs, headmen, and elected members to represent the urban Africans. However, since these boards could only make recommendations and had no powers of implementing their decisions, they ended up being little more than discussion groups.

In 1937 a Native Councils Act was passed which gave the governor the power to appoint African councils with wider powers. These consisted of chiefs, headmen, and others nominated by local communities. The councils dealt with such things as roads, education, and water and were empowered to pass bylaws. In spite of the fact that by 1952 forty-three of these councils had been established, there was little popular support for them. Also in 1937 the chiefs were given slightly wider powers in terms of civil jurisdiction under the African Law and Courts Act. African administration in Southern Rhodesia was thus delegated to some extent to the chiefs, who were appointed by the government, which followed the normal Shona or Ndebele principles of succession whenever it appeared expedient. The appointment and duties of the chiefs fell under the African Affairs Act (1927, amended 1966), and their salaries and allowances were prescribed by, or fell under, legislation subsidiary to this act. For example, section 5 of the African Affairs Act stated: "the Chief in charge of a tribe shall be appointed by the Governor and shall hold office during pleasure and contingent upon good behavior and general fitness. He shall rank as a constable within his tribal area and may be paid such salary and allowances as may from time to time be prescribed by regulations."

It was becoming quite apparent that the administration of Africans posed enormous problems which the small force of native commissioners could not deal with, and the efforts to extend the powers of the chiefs and to establish the councils were attempts at solving these problems. The fusion of democratically elected councils with traditional leaders, however, proved unsuccessful:

It was not long before the policy of developing democratically elected councils, which it was believed would meet the need for political expression and provide younger, more progressive men, to offset the conservatism of the aged chiefs, clashed with the attempt to bolster up the powers of an hereditary office. In many areas, chiefs refused to cooperate with the councils which they claimed were undermining their authority; and so councils in many areas became defunct or were brought to a standstill.[9]

In addition, the Native Trade and Production Commission of 1944 concluded that efforts to increase the powers of the chiefs had also failed. In 1951 the whole institution was reorganized; many chieftainships which were either inoperative or too small to be efficient were abolished, and the salaries and allowances paid to chiefs were revised.

In 1957 the African Councils Act was introduced to expand the earlier concept of councils. The major new feature was the requirement that councils were only to be established where there were definite local requests for them.[10] Members would be elected to the councils once these demands had been articulated, and they would have a right to impose taxes and to fulfill the functions of the earlier councils—roadbuilding, education, and so on. The specific forms of the councils varied from area to area according to local needs. By the end of 1962 there were fifty-five in existence.

[9] Garbett, "The Chief's Dilemma," p. 7.

[10] In 1962 a policy of community development was introduced as an extension of this concept. Despite the fact that the RF made frequent references to the idea of such a policy, there was little concrete evidence of its implementation.

From 1957 onward, efforts were made not only to utilize the chiefs in the bureaucracy but to draw them more directly into the Rhodesian political system as an antidote to the growing influence of the Nationalists. In 1961 the Councils of Chiefs and Provincial Assemblies Act revamped the existing councils yet again and provided for the establishment of provincial assemblies. Under this act the chiefs were provided with direct access to the central government without first passing through the commissioners. Furthermore, in response to the findings of the Mangwende and Robinson Commissions, the native commissioner system was reorganized. The commissioners were renamed "district officers," and they were relieved of some of their judicial duties because these were felt to clash with their administrative ones. Furthermore, they were no longer to handle agricultural and animal-husbandry problems, and they were instructed to persuade rather than order those under their control. The chiefs were now in a position to exert pressure directly on the government and the central administration, and they soon realized this. The channel of communication which formerly had run from the chiefs through the district commissioners had been altered by the introduction of assemblies. At the same time, chiefs now had bargaining power since the government sought desperately to win their support.

Ndebele chiefs have used their improved status far more widely than Shona chiefs. Part of the explanation for this goes back to the early approaches of the native commissioners. Herbert L. Spiro has written of a kind of tribal favoritism in which some native commissioners referred to the Shona as "curs" who had always been inferior to the allegedly more martial and sportsmanlike Ndebele.[11] Also, the Ndebele chiefs are, on the whole, younger than Shona chiefs; and they are somewhat better educated because succession by primogeniture enabled the government to identify the heir and educate him to his duties.

The alliance between the Rhodesian Front and some of the chiefs is not difficult to understand. Both have a vested interest in the perpetuation of the white system; the world outlook of both is inherently conservative; and both are threatened by African nationalism. The government sees in the chiefs a legitimizing of its paternalistic role and a means of retaining some control of the rural areas. The powers of individual chiefs have, therefore, been extended far beyound the concept of authority in either Shona or Ndebele traditional society. Also, to hold the allegiance of the chiefs, salaries have risen far in excess of the annual African wage (a chief with five hundred followers or more was paid £420 per annum, and one with less than five hundred, £240).[12] "In the rural areas, they are being drawn deeply into the RF control network; and their good salaries and ever-increasing powers, both over land and law, make them a formidable force to fear, if not respect."[13] The former minister of internal affairs, William Harper, spelled out some of these powers: The chief is head of the Tribal Land Authority and hence controls the use, allocation, and conservation of land, and

[11] Herbert L. Spiro, "The Rhodesias and Nyasaland," in *Five African States: Responses to Diversity,* Gwendolen M. Carter, ed. (Ithaca: Cornell University Press, 1963), p. 392.

[12] *Hansard,* July 21, 1965.

[13] Larry Bowman, "Rhodesia Since UDI," *Africa Report,* Feb. 1967, p. 12.

as head of the local tribunal court he has jurisdiction in criminal cases.[14] Chiefs, with the aid of assessors, already had civil jurisdiction in these courts.

It is necessary, however, to draw a distinction between the chiefs as a group, used by the Rhodesian Front government as a bolster to specific claims and policies, and the day-to-day operational relationships between the chiefs and the central government. On a broad ideological level, the chiefs are characterized by the white system as "steadfastly loyal to the government . . . the true leaders of the people in the face of challenges to their authority from irresponsible quarters. All this has strengthened their resolution to cooperate with the forces of law and order, which in turn [has] consolidated support for the traditional institutions they represent." [15]

The Domboshawa Indaba of 1964 is perhaps the best example of the Rhodesian Front's use of the chiefs to legitimize its own position. British Prime Minister Wilson had stated that the independence issue should be presented to the Rhodesian people as a whole in an open referendum and that his government would seriously take into account the views thus expressed. The Rhodesian government met part of this demand by calling an Indaba (a council or meeting of chiefs) at Domboshawa, near Salisbury, on October 26, 1964, "preferring the Indaba system as a more appropriate method of ascertaining the views of the mass of tribal Africans than alien practices which the British government and others desire to force the people to accept

[14] *Rhodesia Herald,* Aug. 24, 1967.

[15] *Report of the Secretary for Internal Affairs for the Year 1964* (Salisbury: Government Printer, 1965), p. 4.

in the guise of the vote."[16] In view of the chiefs' dependent role in the Rhodesian system, it is not surprising that they gave a unanimous vote of confidence to the government for a possible Unilateral Declaration of Independence. William Harper summed it up in saying:

> I have listened to you and it seems to me that you have already taken a decision in this matter. It seems to me that the chiefs and headmen are all of one mind and your decision is to cut the strings without delay. I must ask, however, that if any of you would like to speak against the decision that he be invited to do so now. [No reply.] You have decided, obviously in your own way as to how this decision has been taken.[17]

But the chief must also be seen at the intersection of two political systems. He is the highest political authority in the traditional system, yet he occupies one of the lowest roles in the Rhodesian bureaucracy. In their attempts to reconcile conflicting expectations, the chiefs either fade into the background and become ineffectual in the eyes of the government because they neglect the administrative side of their office, or they are openly compromised in the eyes of their people. Thus, for example, in the period from 1944 to 1964, nineteen chiefs were deposed by the government, and in the major reorganization of the institution in 1951, eighty-nine chieftainships (out of 321—27 per cent) were completely abolished, and forty-one chiefs (12 per cent) were reduced to subchiefs.[18]

In 1957, in the case of *Muwuungani* v. *Minister of Na-*

[16] *The Domboshawa "Indaba": The Demand for Independence for Rhodesia (Consultation with African Tribesmen through Their Chiefs and Headmen)* (Salisbury: Government Printer, 1964), p. 15.
[17] *Ibid.*, p. 33. [18] *Rhodesia Herald*, Feb. 22, 1964.

*tive Affairs,* the chief justice, Sir Robert Tredgold, remarked that the African tribes in Rhodesia were in no way identifiable with those that existed prior to the European presence, but were rather administrative units created by administrative action under the African Affairs Act.[19] In 1963, the Patterson Commission, which examined the Rhodesian public services, included the following report from a district officer: "It is absurd to claim that the chiefs are still the leaders of their people, as if it were true for all chiefs and that other leaders were non-existent. The dangers of political leaders would not be there if the leadership of the chiefs were so firm, so deep, so certain, as some claim." [20]

Although the government is anxious to utilize the chiefs and to extend their authority, many chiefs are unable to live up to the expectations of the modern bureaucracy of which they are a part. As a consequence, both modern (i.e., nationalist) and traditional leadership are vitiated by severe limitations imposed on them by the white government.

## *The Chiefs in the Senate*

Under the 1969 constitution, there were to be ten chiefs elected by the National Council of Chiefs to the Rhodesian Senate. This opened up new possibilities for African political participation, considering the potentially powerful position of the chiefs within Rhodesian politics. The involvement of the chiefs in the Senate in the political pro-

[19] *Muwuungani* v. *Minister of Native Affairs, South African Law Reports* (Cape Town: Juta, 1957).

[20] *Second Report of the Commission of Enquiry Into the Organization and Development of Southern Rhodesia Public Service* (Salisbury: Government Printer, 1963), p. 18.

cess, however, seldom went beyond what might be referred to as "naïve politics." When chiefs took initiative, the new issues they introduced were primarily focused on minor rural problems. The chiefs often merely provided an apparent aura of legitimacy for pre-existing government policy, or served a ceremonial role. Senator Chief Kayisa, for example, agreed with the government's policy on immigration, perceived of Rhodesia as a country "peaceful more than any country that I know of," and emphasized that the chiefs were the leaders of the African people in Rhodesia.[21] Senator Chief Mugabe made a statement which must indeed have been satisfying to the paternalistic policies of the Rhodesian Front Party: "I would like to thank our present government who have the courage to work with all the people of Rhodesia who will stand with them—the Prime Minister Mr. Smith, his ministers, all members of the Parliament, and all the people who have the welfare of this country at heart. I am very happy to be Rhodesian." [22]

Senator Chiefs Mafala and Ndiweni devoted considerable time and energy to rural issues. For example, Senator Mafala was concerned with the taxing of farm vehicles.[23] Other senators devoted attention to the question of African education in both the urban and the rural areas. Senator Chief Sigola, whom many perceived of as the

21 *Hansard,* June 2, 1970.

22 *Ibid.,* June 3, 1970. Similar sentiments were expressed by Senator Chief Mzimuni: "The first thing I wish to do is to thank the President of our country for all the work that he is doing in our country. He is certainly a great leader of men and we have seen that he is a good and thoughtful leader. Another thing I wish to thank him for is the way he travels around our country with his good lady so that the people can see him, and it shows in a very real way that he loves his people" (*ibid.,* June 1, 1971).

23 *Ibid.,* June 3, 1970.

leader of the chiefs in the Senate, emphasized technical education, preparing Africans with special skills.[24] On African education, Senator Ndiweni presented a very practical view: "We want to see the children in these areas learn more practical work, like carpentry, building, plumbing and electrical work, so that they can also become surveyors and motor mechanics. . . . At this time, the emphasis of the present training is centered around the idea of leading [students] on to the universities." [25] This view was backed by Senator Chief Sogwala, who called for greater government involvement in technical education in Africa. The chiefs were also concerned with the lack of industry in the rural sectors, and it is not surprising to find that they advocated an equivalent policy to that of the South African border industries, where the government encouraged white industries to build plants on the borders of areas reserved for Africans. Senator Chief Ndiweni was thus "pleased to hear the Minister of Internal Affairs say that he thinks that all the work like industry in the towns should move out into the Tribal Trust Lands." [26]

The chiefs on the whole were highly critical of anyone who challenged their authority, Senator Chief Ngorima going so far as to maintain: "The Bible says that the Chief is the hand of God and those who do wrong should be dealt with by him." [27] Chief Ngorima was also critical of the activity of the nationalist organizations such as ZAPU. It is interesting to note that both Chiefs Ndiweni and Sigola strongly objected to Africans being excluded from military conscription.[28]

[24] *Ibid.*, June 2, 1971.
[25] *Ibid.*, Aug. 5, 1970.
[26] *Ibid.*, Aug. 12, 1970.
[27] *Ibid.*, Aug. 13, 1970.
[28] *Ibid.*, Sept. 30, 1970.

On rare occasions some chiefs were critical of government policies. Senator Chief Ndiweni spoke out against "people who have been moved from their original places, moved to new areas. I cannot really follow government's policy on this. . . . I do not really agree with the policies of removing people from the areas where they have been born and brought up." [29] He also voiced the suspicion that African produce was not being included in export projects and was concerned about Rhodesian agriculture falling under two different ministries, one European and one African. He was particularly concerned that African farmers in the Tribal Trust Land were not being aided by the Agriculture Development Authority. "I ask that all agriculture, whether European or African, should be put under one ministry to enable all farmers of Rhodesia to progress." [30] As far as the urban areas were concerned, Chief Sigola and Chief Ndiweni expressed concern over the lack of African participation in the control of African townships.[31]

The interdependence of the chiefs and the RF government is well illustrated in debate over the African Marriages Bill, which provided that in those districts in which chiefs were to be appointed marriage officers by the minister of internal affairs people would not need to go to the district commissioner's office for the registration or solemnization of their marriages. Several African members of Parliament in the lower house ironically disapproved of this extension of the powers of the chiefs. But the chiefs were excited about regaining prestige and power at a time when their own people were not providing them with

[29] *Ibid.,* June 13, 1970. [30] *Ibid.,* March 17, 1971.
[31] *Ibid.,* March 13, 1971.

traditional respect. As elsewhere, the Rhodesian government was artificially attempting to provide the chiefs with a new sense of dignity and power. The relationship was, therefore, mutually advantageous: the chiefs regained stature—albeit artificial stature—and the RF government substantiated its paternalistic claims.

The sphere of operation and of influence of the chiefs in the Senate was, quite clearly, extremely limited. They must be largely perceived as an expensive rubber stamp. The salaries paid to them as senators, their parliamentary allowances, the expensive facilities for simultaneous translation of speeches into Shona, Sindebele, and English, only resulted in platitudes of support and the restating of obvious rural problems. But the Rhodesian government needed the chiefs as their primary legitimizing agents in their claim of solid African support. "They are no more paid servants of government than the elected members on both sides of the House of Commons are—even though, like members of Parliament, they can be removed from office with certain misdemeanors," stated the official *Rhodesian Commentary*. "Conscious of this knowledge the Rhodesian government respects them, encourages them to play their traditionally vital part, and accepts 'the voice of the tribe' to achieve peace and progress under stable government." [32]

The value of the Senate was perhaps summed up by Senator Chief Ndiweni. "I think the Senate itself is an example of good race relations and an example for everybody to see. Last year we worked very well and close together. I can see no reason why the peoples of Rhodesia should not get to see the race relations which were established last year continue in the years to come. . . . a house

[32] *Rhodesian Commentary,* March 4, 1968.

divided amongst itself will fall." [33] But, ironically, the chiefs themselves were in practice part of the African house divided, and failure to recognize this fact was one of the fundamental tragedies of Rhodesian politics.

It is not surprising that in 1972 the chiefs in the Senate were quick to give unanimous support to the Anglo-Rhodesian settlement proposals and strongly recommended that all Africans support them. So did the National Council of Chiefs with which the commissioners met in January 1972. Twenty-four of the twenty-six members of the council were present (two were ill at the time). The meeting lasted for five and a half hours and took place in the Salisbury High Court building. According to the Pearce Commission Report, the meeting was conducted "formally, but in privacy." [34] The chiefs told the commission that they represented 230 senior chiefs, 400 headmen, and 28,000 *kraal* (village) heads. They emphasized that they were not "stooges" and that the commission should accept their opinion rather than those expressed in the towns.

When the chiefs met the commissioners in the tribal areas, however, their position altered radically; some of the members still supported the settlement proposals, but others, seen either alone or with other people in their tribal areas, gave a "no" vote. Out of a total of 245 chiefs, 184 were seen by the commission; 44 accepted the proposals, 87 rejected them, and 53 abstained from an opinion. In addition, twenty letters were received from chiefs, six

[33] *Hansard,* June 2, 1971.

[34] Great Britain Cmnd. 4964 (1972), *Rhodesia: Report of the Commission on Rhodesian Opinion under the Chairmanship of the Right Honourable Lord Pearce,* p. 26.

in favor of and fourteen against the proposals. Perhaps the most telling statement on the whole matter of the involvement of chiefs is found in the Pearce Commission Report. "Many Chiefs seem to be acutely embarrassed by the demand that they should express a political opinion at all." [35]

[35] *Ibid.*, p. 49.

CHAPTER 6

# African Nationalism: Attempts to Achieve Constitutional Reform

Early African nationalist movements in Rhodesia operated within the political system and sought reforms on a constitutional basis. However, because of the reluctance of the white establishment to broaden its bases of support and the polarized nature of Rhodesian society, a more rigid and permanent dichotomy developed over time. The white power structure was reluctant to permit reforms aimed at increasing African participation, and, in addition, it limited channels of protest and opportunities for mobilization. Inevitably, therefore, the Nationalists eventually moved beyond the basic operational codes and tried to establish new rules of the game. To the degree they ceased to operate within the prevailing system, a "turbulent" political situation developed in which opponents were regarded as enemies.[1]

## *Nationalist Movements within the Rhodesian System*

Protonationalist organizations existed in Rhodesia from as early as the 1920's.[2] Until that time the African Na-

[1] See Giovanni Sartori, "Opposition and Control: Problems and Prospects," *Government and Opposition,* 1, no. 2 (Feb. 1966).

[2] There were other organizations of a more limited nature. For example, the Mandabele Patriotic Society, or Loyal Mandabele Society, which was primarily concerned with Mandabele people and dealt with the decay of traditional values, was founded in 1916. The

tionalists in South Africa watched over the interests of the Rhodesian Africans. One of the earliest indigenous organizations was the Rhodesian Native Association (RNA), which concentrated on the villages and farms of Mashonaland. In 1920 the chief native commissioner described it as "a reputable organization not associated with those organizations of South Africa wanting Africa for the Africans." [3] In the early years its leaders included Z. A. Chivuumta, J. S. Mokwile, S. Matabese, a Xhosa missionary, and Walter Chipwaya. It primarily sought to operate on behalf of an educated elite, and at all times was concerned with constitutional politics. The aims of the RNA included the obtaining of "certificates of exemption" to free educated Africans from the operation of the Pass Laws, and it also planned to send a delegation to interview General Smuts (the prime minister of South Africa) on the terms for Rhodesia's incorporation into the Union of South Africa.

In 1922, Abraham Twala, a Zulu from South Africa who was teaching for the Anglican Church in Rhodesia, started making plans for a new African organization. He was assisted by Ernest Dube, Thomas Maziyani, and Garner Sojini, a Fingo, also from South Africa.[4] The immediate concern of these men was the forthcoming referendum on

---

society exhorted its members to "tell the father or guardian of the fallen women to report them to the native commissioner or police; if you know any bad house, point it out to the English detectives; honour the king and respect his laws."

[3] Nathan M. Shamuyarira, *Crisis in Rhodesia* (London: Andre Deutsch, 1965), p. 31.

[4] There was a marked absence of Shona in this organization; its leadership was primarily Ndebele.

responsible government; they wanted to see a continued British presence rather than the establishment of links with South Africa. The first meeting of the Rhodesia Bantu Voters' Association (RBVA) took place on January 20, 1923,[5] under the chairmanship of Ernest Dube. Among those who participated in the organization, in addition to those already mentioned, were Stuart Sojini, of Selukwe; Martha Ngano, Bulawayo; Eli Nare, Salisbury.

In its constitution, issued in July 1923, the RBVA maintained that it would attempt to "safeguard the interest of the Bantu people domiciled in Rhodesia; to be a medium of expression of representative opinion and to formulate a standard policy on Native Affairs for the guidance of the Parliament [Legislative Council]; and to endevour to secure co-operation with the 'Powers that be' and all others interested in the advancement of the Bantu peoples without laying an embargo in their way."[6] Its motto was: "Honour all men. Love the Brotherhood. Fear God. Honour the King."[7] Like the RNA, it saw itself operating in order to change, rather than to supplant, the political system. In operational terms, the work of the association was to be effected and advanced by means of resolutions and constitutional and peaceful propaganda; by consulting the Native Affairs Department, missionaries, and other officials who are interested or in a position to advise; by appealing to the highest constitutional tribunal; and by distributing literature and holding lectures to educate

[5] By this time they were too late to make a decisive impact on the referendum.

[6] Clause 4, Rhodesian Bantu Voters' Association Constitution, July 1923, Rhodesian Archives.

[7] Shamuyarira, *Crisis in Rhodesia,* p. 31.

the public as well as the Bantu thus affected.[8] Members of the organization were concerned with politically educating the elite, providing educational facilities, obtaining the right to own or purchase land, the right to vote, and exemptions from the inconveniences of the Pass system.

Members had to be over eighteen years of age and paid an initial enrollment fee of 5 shillings and thereafter an annual fee of 2/6 or 1/6, depending on whether they were registered voters or not. It is interesting to note that members included the chief native commissioner and the superintendent of natives. By 1924 a branch office had been established in Bulawayo under the energetic control of Martha Ngano.

In 1934, Aaron Jaca founded Southern Rhodesia's first African National Congress, patterned on nationalist organizations in South Africa. It concentrated for its membership on unenfranchised urban dwellers and continually worked within the prevailing Rhodesian system.[9] It attempted to improve the position of the educated urban African by means of petitions and consultation with the white authorities. Its tone was moderate, and while objecting to the Pass Laws (which required adult male Africans to register with the native commissioner at the age of fourteen and to carry registration certificates [*situpa*]) and the Maize Control Act (which discriminated against African farmers in favor of small white growers) its representatives had informed the Bledisloe Commission that there was no complaint with the Land Apportionment Act.[10]

[8] Clause 5, Rhodesian Bantu Voters' Association Constitution, July 1923, Rhodesian Archives.

[9] Shamuyarira, *Crisis in Rhodesia,* p. 31.

[10] A. J. Wills, *An Introduction to the History of Central Africa* (London: Oxford University Press, 1964), p. 253.

This organization had little impact on the white establishment. By 1938 it had only 150 members.

One of the most significant events in the period from 1920 to 1945 was the establishment in South Africa of the Industrial and Commercial Workers' Union (ICU) by Thomas Sambo. In the 1920's the ICU began to open branches in Southern Rhodesia. It was a social, political, and welfare organization rather than a trade union in the strictest sense. Politically, it focused attention on what it referred to as "the three-legged stool" of the white establishment—the Land Apportionment Act, the Industrial Conciliation Act[11] and the Native Registration Act. Masothsha Ndhlovu, Thomas Sikaleni, and Charles Mzingeli all played prominent leadership roles in the ICU, Mzingeli, in particular, in the Bulawayo area from about 1927 onward. In 1929 the chief native commissioner commented:

The problems of the Union of South Africa, especially those of the industrial sort, have their repercussions in this Colony, mainly in the formation of attempts at religious separatism. The Industrial and Commercial Workers' Union has its emissaries who are very active in endeavours to promote discontent among native workers at industrial centers. The methods employed (borrowed from the South) are those of agitators in Hyde Park, and consist in denouncing the Government, the laws, the European and native officials, European employers and the wages paid by them. The movement is in its infancy and has made little headway so far, but it has dangerous possibilities, chief of which is the spreading of a contempt for law and order into the presently quiet and contented homes of the people. . . . In this regard the Native Commissioner, Salis-

[11] This act created a color bar in the field of skilled employment.

bury, remarks: "The I.C.U. has established a branch in Salisbury and is endeavouring to cause trouble between the European and native races. It seems unfortunate that a hitherto contented people should be led astray by agitators who are paid to stir up strife."

The commissioner concluded by remarking that "in spite of active propaganda it is reported from Bulawayo that the powder train of real conviction has not yet caught fire." [12]

J. Van Velsen has perceptively concluded that these early associations "tended to be run and to appeal to the new African elite who were greatly concerned to gain from the whites social recognition as 'advanced natives' in contrast to the 'uneducated masses.' The end attitudes of these early associations clearly imply that they were resigned to white rule and had committed themselves to many aspects of a new European-modelled way of life." [13]

The RNA and the RBVA were not parties in the sense of representation, conversion and aggregation, integration, persuasion, policy formation, and control of government; they were minimally effective pressure groups recruiting both leaders and members either from the urban elite or from distinct ethnic groups. In connection with these African organizations, T. O. Ranger maintained that by the mid 1920's Southern Rhodesia had three modern-style African political associations.[14] He goes on further to state that these associations failed in their attempts to

[12] *Report of the Chief Native Commissioner for the Year 1929* (Salisbury: Government Printer, 1929), pp. 1, 12.

[13] J. Van Velsen, "Trends in African Nationalism in Southern Rhodesia," *Kroniek van Afrika* (Leiden), 2 (June 1964), p. 141.

[14] Terence O. Ranger, *The African Voice in Southern Rhodesia, 1898–1930* (London: Heinemann, 1970), p. 226.

modify the responsible government system by working within it. Whenever a dangerous alliance formed between the town dwellers and the rural sectors,[15] the authorities immediately expressed disapproval sufficient to break up the organizations.[16] In addition, Ranger examines other political maneuvers such as the limit on the expansion of movements, dismissal of men from jobs, police deportations, prosecutions and advice to chiefs not to mix with political agitators.

Protonationalist organizations had distinct undertones of nationalist sentiment but operated on a restricted level in both recruitment of members and political action. Their main importance is the basis they provided for the modern movements—a set of policies for articulating grievances and events that set the parameters of confrontation.

## *African Nationalism since 1945*

In Southern Rhodesia, as in other parts of Africa, World War II led to increased African urbanization and an expanded African political consciousness. The British African Voice Association was formed in 1947, and until it was banned in 1952, it was led by Benjamin Burumbo. The organization operated mainly in urban centers such as Salisbury and Bulawayo, and perceived of itself in constitutional terms, focusing on the social, economic, and

[15] Religious groups also were involved in political activities. The Watchtower movements were important because they attempted to provide a supernatural solution to the African predicament. Because of their religious dimensions, however, they were in a different genre than the RNA, the RBVA, and the ANC.

[16] The Rhodesian government was most favorable to the RNA, more critical of the RBVA, and opposed to the ICU.

industrial needs of Africans. It saw itself as an intermediary between the white government and Africans, and according to its constitution would do "all things that may be necessary or desirable to advance Africa in civilization." [17]

Also in the 1940's African nationalist protest began to take the form of party politics for the first time; the Reverend T. D. Samkange assumed the leadership of what has now come to be known as "the old ANC"—the old African National Congress—which sought the repeal of discriminatory legislation, such as the Pass Laws, but had limited success in achieving its ends.

In the early 1950's powerful labor movements dominated African politics, especially the Reformed Industrial Council of Unions (RICU), under the leadership of Charles Mzingeli.[18] Joshua Nkomo was at the time general secretary of another union, the Railway African Workers Union; others involved in this organization were Michael Mawema, Jason Moyo, and John Chirimbani, all later to become prominent in nationalist organizations. The African Teachers' Association had members such as Ndabaningi Sithole, Robert Mugabe, and Leopold Takawira. Ultimately, the union movements failed because the white power structure refused to participate in any form of bargaining with them and used force whenever they felt the movements were getting out of hand.

In August 1955 an important development took place. The Youth League (YL) was established by Edson Sithole, Dunduza Chisiza, Henry Hamadziripi, and Stanley

[17] Article I, Constitution of the British African Voice Association, Rhodesian Archives.

[18] These labor movements flourished despite the fact that they had to contend with obstacles such as the migrant labor system and its shifting effect on membership and contributions.

Parirewa;[19] the president of the organization was James Chikerema. At first they modeled the Youth League on the Sukarno Youth Movement in Indonesia and attempted to secretly infiltrate into urban and rural areas. However, George Nyandoro of the Capricorn Africa Society guided it toward the general direction of the trade unions and utilized mass movements to bring pressure on the government, such as a successful mass bus boycott in Harare Township in Salisbury in 1957. On September 12, 1957, the leadership of the Youth League called for a meeting of all organized African political or quasi-political groups throughout the country. As a result of the meeting, a new African National Congress (ANC) was born under the leadership of Joshua Nkomo.

The ANC emphasized a nonracial political philosophy; white Rhodesians were welcome to join the ANC, although they felt a different title should be used because the term "African" seemed to exclude members of other races. Joshua Nkomo, however, said that the words "African" and "National" applied to all peoples in Rhodesia, and he hoped that all races would support the organization. At the outset, Africans with the necessary franchise qualifications were encouraged to register on the voters' roll. Nyandoro referred to India's struggle and hoped that the example of Ghandi would be followed. The ANC decided to operate on a constitutional level by means of petitions to ministers, public protests, and memoranda to the government. Among its direct concerns were the establishment of a policy of one man–one vote, opposition to discriminatory legislation, and opposition to the Native Land Husbandry Act of 1951.

[19] See Shamuyarira, *Crisis in Rhodesia,* pp. 39–42.

In addition to breaking down national racial barriers the ANC hoped to overcome any existing ethnic differences within the organization. Indeed, from the beginning several whites, Asians, and Coloureds became members. The motto of the ANC was "Forwards ever, backward never."

The ANC went into operation in both the urban and rural areas and had particular success in mobilizing African farmers in 1959 against the Native Land Husbandry Act in what it referred to as "Operation Sunrise." The Land Husbandry Act aimed at reform in farming methods by means of destocking and the introduction of individual ownership to agricultural landholding. The act ran contrary to the traditional concept of communal ownership and to the status of cattle within traditional society. Because of the ANC's ability to capitalize on the discontent of African farmers, George Nyandoro of the ANC commented: "The Land Husbandry Act has been the best recruiter Congress ever had." [20] The minister of justice and law and order at the time, Reginald Knight, conservatively estimated that there were 6,000 to 7,000 African members of the ANC.[21] Others [22] consider that there were as many as 250,000 paid-up members and that branches of the party, such as the Harare branch and the branch at Highfield, were collecting as much as £500 a week in subscriptions.

It was because of the potentially strong rural base rather than its large-scale urban support (which was more of a

[20] As cited in B. V. Mtshali, *Rhodesia: Background to Conflict* (New York: Hawthorn Books, 1967), p. 69.

[21] *Evening Standard* (Salisbury), April 15, 1959.

[22] For example, Davis M'Gabe in *Africa Report,* Feb. 1967, p. 19.

known quantity) that Sir Edgar Whitehead banned the ANC in February 1959. The minister of native affairs, Jack Quinton, clearly stated that members of the congress were undermining recognized authority in the rural areas: "Congress officials had been visiting these areas where recognized authority is being undermined by Congress agitation. Typical of this is the Mangwende Reserve. Here according to reports, unrest and ill-feeling are mounting as a result of the struggle for power between Congress and the Reserve Council." [23]

After the ANC was banned there was no real underground operation to sustain what had been a grass-roots response to a particular problem. The ANC had provided a means of political expression for Africans who, until that time, felt entirely excluded from the political process. Few had had direct contact with members of Parliament or with any white authorities. The ANC clearly marked the beginning of a process of mass political education for Southern Rhodesian Africans.

Sir Edgar Whitehead made the parameters of African political participation absolutely clear at a meeting in Bulawayo in December 1959. He said that while he could imagine an African political party which showed no trace of extremism, as soon as the mainspring of the party became nationalist it would almost inevitably become militant. "Another African nationalist organization in Southern Rhodesia of a militant nature such as the African Congress would be completely fatal to the whole conception of partnership." In his view, it would certainly provoke into existence a European nationalist organization.

[23] *Rhodesia Herald,* Feb. 4, 1959.

"If one race starts this sort of thing, then the other will follow suit, and then a clash becomes inevitable." [24]

The year 1959 also marked the passage of the Unlawful Organizations Act and the Preventive Detention Act. Some prominent Africans were still participating in the political system. For example, Leopold Takawira, who was among those who discussed the need for a new nationalist organization, was at the time a member of the executive of the Capricorn Africa Society. Others felt that support should be given to Garfield Todd's Central African Party.

On January 1, 1960, Michael Mawema formed the National Democratic Party (NDP). Its aims were to serve as a vigorous vanguard for removing all forms of oppression and for the establishment of a democratic government in Southern Rhodesia; to work for speedy constitutional reconstruction in Southern Rhodesia—with the object of having a government elected on the premise of one man–one vote; to work for the educational, political, social, and economic emancipation of the people; and to work with other democratic movements in Africa and the rest of the world to abolish colonial racism and all forms of racial oppression and economic inequality among nations. According to Mawema, the NDP sought majority rule, higher wages for Africans, land for people displaced by the Native Land Husbandry Act, facilities for the education of African children, and better housing in the urban areas.[25] To a large extent the NDP emphasized an urban rather than a rural struggle. Above all, in its early stages, the NDP was concerned with constitutional reform and committed itself to this end in its constitution. The party had a large repre-

[24] *Ibid.*, Dec. 12, 1959.

[25] *African Daily News*, July 25, 1960.

sentation of African intellectuals—Enoch Dumbutshena; Stanlake Samkange, Herbert Chitepo, the first Southern Rhodesian African advocate; two medical doctors, Tichafa Parirenyatwa and E. M. Pswarayi; Bernard Chidzero, who had a Ph.D. in political science from McGill University; George Silundika, Robert Mugabe, and Leopold Takawira. This was the first time that so many of the elite had become involved in the leadership of nationalist politics.

In April 1960, Michael Mawema met with the commonwealth relations secretary, Lord Home, to request that the British government retain the reserved clauses which protected African rights and call a constitutional conference which would include African leaders, to discuss the future of Southern Rhodesia.

In July 1960, however, the arrests of Michael Mawema, Sketchley Samkange, and Leopold Takawira led to large-scale demonstrations in Salisbury and Bulawayo. Sir Edgar Whitehead opposed the NDP because it aimed at one man–one vote and sought to negotiate directly with Great Britain. He saw it as the ANC in a new guise and hence tried to hamper its activities. Those arrested were charged under the Unlawful Organizations Act, specifically section 10 of the act, which states: "If any books, accounts, writings, papers, documents, banners of insignia of, or relating to, an unlawful organization are found in the possession or under the control of any person or if any person wears insignia of or is marked with any marks of an unlawful organization, it shall be presumed, until the contrary is proved, that such a person is a member of that organization."

Sir Edgar Whitehead felt that if he could prove that the

NDP was the ANC in a new form, the NDP would become an unlawful organization and he could end its growth by arresting its leaders. But he had underestimated both African mass support for the NDP and its reaction to the arrests. At a mass meeting on July 19 in Highfield, George Silundika, while emphasizing nonviolence, told everyone in the crowd to go to the Highfield police station and surrender themselves as a token of support for those leaders who had been arrested; they should publicly proclaim that they too were members of an unlawful organization. A crowd estimated at between 30,000 and 40,000 persons then assembled near the Stoddart Hall in Harare, where it was stopped by a police barrier and remained overnight. Some of the nationalist leaders requested that Sir Edgar Whitehead meet with them at this point. When it became clear that he was not going to do so, the crowd once again tried to move toward the center of the city but were held back by a police barrier. Two of the leaders then made their way to Parliament to meet Whitehead, who refused to see them. He called up members of the First Battalion of the Royal Rhodesian Regiment and banned all meetings in Harare. Police eventually broke up the Salisbury crowd. On July 25, rioting in Bulawayo led to thirteen African deaths and considerable damage to property.

This was the time of Sir Edgar Whitehead's Constitutional Conference to which, in October 1960, Nkomo, while abroad, was elected as the head of the NDP delegation. This in itself was something of a victory, since Whitehead had initially not invited an NDP delegation but had asked Herbert Chitepo to attend as an individual. Chitepo refused to do this, at which point commonwealth relations secretary Duncan Sandys, with considerable difficulty, persuaded Whitehead to include a formal delegation from the NDP.

The meetings between the Nationalists, the Rhodesian government, and the British government took place in February 1961 in Salisbury, under the chairmanship of Duncan Sandys, and at first resulted in an agreement on new constitutional proposals. After consultation with members of the NDP executive, however, Nkomo withdrew his support, and in October 1961, the congress of the NDP decided not to participate in the election.

This decision has been the source of considerable controversy ever since. Some political observers consider that the NDP should have fought the election. This would have given it a firm constitutional base within Parliament and, at the same time, enabled it to organize on a large scale outside of Parliament. But many members of the NDP felt at the time that it was not worth contesting the fifteen seats set aside for Africans, since this would not give them a sufficiently wide political base.

The NDP had to operate under severe disadvantages; for example, its members were forbidden to organize in the rural areas, mass meetings were discouraged by different municipalities, members of the executive were harassed by both the police and the provisions of the Law and Order (Maintenance) Act. In addition, the group was plagued with organizational difficulties. Among its achievements, nonetheless, were the Constitutional Conference and the repeal of the Native Land Husbandry Act and of laws requiring discrimination in certain public places (cinemas, hotels, and so on).

In the end, however, African leaders had come to realize that none of the reforms for which they were pressing

—in particular, majority rule—could be achieved without real political power and that as long as the white minority had control of the sources of power, they could not achieve their ends.

CHAPTER 7

# African Nationalism: The Years of Conflict, 1961 to the Present

Sir Edgar Whitehead was caught in a difficult position in 1961. On the one hand, he realized that the Nationalists had valid grievances and that they would continue to reorganize; while there were new names for the parties, the central leadership core remained unchanged—only the radicalism with which it approached political problems varied. He also understood that finding a solution to the problem of African aspirations was viscerally linked with the constitutional issue of Rhodesian independence. On the other hand, the white electorate was beginning to demand a tougher policy in regard to the Nationalists. The NDP was banned in August 1961. From 1962 onward, the lines were more clearly drawn: the confrontation was becoming one between white and black nationalism.

The National Democratic Party re-emerged as the Zimbabwe African People's Union (ZAPU) in December 1961, again under the leadership of Joshua Nkomo. The growing dichotomy between ZAPU and the establishment is evidenced by the following statements. Sir Edgar Whitehead felt that if ZAPU "wishes to fight this new constitution there is no other way of fighting it except through Parliament that would be acceptable."[1] Dr. Tichafa Parirenyatwa, deputy president of ZAPU, countered: "The

[1] *Rhodesia Herald,* Dec. 18, 1961.

new constitution will be wrecked if there is no substantial number of African voters when the first election of African voters takes place in October this year." [2]

As early as January 1961, the late Dr. Parirenyatwa had put forward a sharply opposed position: "ZAPU considers it essential to set aside the new Southern Rhodesian Constitution as a prerequisite for a new deal. It will therefore organize intensively against the voter registration campaign which, by placing a few Africans on the lower roll and reserving the upper roll for Europeans, is meant to deceive the outside world into believing that the African has now a substantial measure of participation in the running of his country when in reality about 99 percent of the total African population will be excluded." [3] Robert Mugabe of ZAPU maintained in December 1961 that "there is no purpose in taking part because the chance of improvement in the franchise is very limited. We can exert extraparliamentary pressure and we believe that is the right course for us at the moment." [4]

ZAPU continued the NDP's attempt to internationalize the Rhodesian struggle.[5] In March and June of 1962, Nkomo visited the United Nations in the hope that pressure could be brought on Britain to convene a new constitutional commission which would give a better deal to Africans. Nkomo was confident that Rhodesia was moving on an irreversible path toward self-determination. The encouragement he received at the U.N., recent events in black Africa, and his strong base of urban support con-

[2] *Ibid.,* Jan. 22, 1962. [3] *Ibid.,* Jan. 8, 1961.
[4] *Evening Standard* (Salisbury), Dec. 21, 1961.
[5] Perhaps because of its lack of success within Rhodesia.

vinced him that the process toward independence could not be turned back. Leopold Takawira, in April of the same year, had promised that ZAPU would take power by 1963.[6]

Shortly thereafter, Ndabaningi Sithole, the national chairman of ZAPU, further stressed this position:

> The new constitution attempts to reverse what has happened in Ghana, Nigeria, in what used to be French West and Equatorial Africa, and free North Africa. It attempts to prevent what has happened in Tanganyika and what is about to happen in Kenya, Uganda, Nyasaland and Northern Rhodesia. In plain language, it purports to prevent the Africans in Southern Rhodesia from getting their freedom and independence as other African countries have done.[7]

This statement sums up ZAPU's expectation that Africans in Rhodesia would ultimately be given their independence as had been the case in other parts of Africa; hence, ZAPU was not prepared to make so great a compromise within the white system and decided to withdraw from the 1962 election.

This withdrawal may be seen as a watershed in the movement toward antisystem politics and eventually into extrasystem politics, with all of its implications of violence and sabotage. ZAPU's objectives indicated the trend toward the conflict inherent in extrasystem politics: (1) to fight for the immediate and total liquidation of imperialism and colonialism, direct or indirect, and to cooperate with any international forces as are engaged in this struggle; (2) to establish a democratic state with a government based on

[6] *Evening Standard,* April 30, 1962.

[7] *Zimbabwe African Peoples Union,* circular no. 2 (June 1962).

one man–one vote and in which democratic liberties thrive; (3) to foster the spirit of Pan-Africanism in Zimbabwe; (4) to maintain peaceful and friendly relations with such nations as are peaceful and friendly; (5) to eliminate economic exploitation and to struggle for economic prosperity in order to achieve the greatest happiness of the greatest number; (6) to foster the best in African culture and thereby develop the basis of desirable social order.[8]

In July 1962 a distinct pattern of violence emerged between the government and African Nationalists. Over the years Africans had shown a remarkable tolerance and spirit of conciliation; in 1962 the use of violence was their only possible response, in most instances, to a system that was becoming increasingly restrictive and stifling. The government had engaged in sporadic violence prior to this date—for example, on January 29, 1962, the police opened fire first on a ZAPU meeting outside the Cyril Jennings Hall at Highfield, Salisbury—but now there was a dramatic increase in both the scope and intensity of the acts by the police. A government White Paper, *The Report on the Zimbabwe African People's Union,* issued in September 1962, listed the types of incidents in which the government claimed Africans were involved: (1) petrol-bomb attacks, mainly against Africans and their homes; (2) criminal acts against Africans, their homes and families; (3) the burning of rural schools; (4) burning or other damage to churches; (5) damage to or interference with communications; (6) attacks on police and police reservists; (7) burning and destruction of buildings used for African amenities or services; (8) attacks against trade union organizations and officials; (9) miscellaneous threats to European-owned prop-

[8] *Rhodesia Herald,* Dec. 18, 1961.

erty; intimidation, and other forms of violence.[9] It is of interest to note that among the houses bombed by ZAPU were those of Patrick Rubatika, P. E. Chigogo, and Josiah Gondo, who were African members of Whitehead's United Federal Party.

The use of violence may be viewed as an effort by ZAPU to create an early crisis in Rhodesia; it may also be seen as an adjunct to Nkomo's efforts to influence international opinion and to add thrust to his direct demands to the British government for independence. ZAPU was banned on September 20, 1962, nine months after it had been formed. All of its leaders were arrested except Nkomo, who was in Lusaka, Northern Rhodesia, at the time.

It must not be forgotten that while this violence by Africans might have been a political tool, it was at the same time an expression of "grievances of very long standing. Poor segregated housing, low wages, shortage of land, destocking of African owned cattle, inadequate education, and last—but not least important—lack of human dignity in one's homeland." [10] "The main feature of ZAPU's short life was a growing conviction among Africans that their struggle would have to involve bloodshed and violence." [11] A second point is that the violence had the continued support of the urban masses: "For nine months ZAPU followed in the footsteps of its predecessor. It gathered thousands upon thousands of faithful supporters. . . . It collected thousands of pounds in donations and subscriptions,

[9] *The Report on the Zimbabwe African People's Union* (Salisbury: Government Printer, 1962), p. 5.

[10] *Chapupu,* Nov. 1962, p. 12.

[11] Nathan M. Shamuyarira, *Crisis in Rhodesia* (London: Andre Deutsch, 1965), p. 72.

and the confiscated scooters of the NDP were replaced by Land Rovers and better sedans." [12]

From the other side, one of the main factors behind the banning of ZAPU was Sir Edgar Whitehead's concern with the prevailing sentiment of the white electorate, especially in the face of the important 1962 general election. The use of violence by ZAPU—though violence exerted mainly against the African community—came at a time when disorders in the Congo were uppermost in the minds of the white electorate. In an effort to safeguard the survival of the UFP, Sir Edgar felt it necessary to follow a hard line.

The growing polarization between the Nationalists and the white establishment is indicated by a letter sent in 1962 by Ndabaningi Sithole (then still on the executive of ZAPU) to all registered African voters:

> Sir Edgar Whitehead is a European leader. He looks after the interests of the whites only. Those Africans who think Sir Edgar Whitehead cares for their interests might as well think that a leopard thinks for the interests of a goat. Sir Edgar was chosen by whites and therefore he is responsible only to whites. Make no mistake about this. In 1959 they asked him to ban the ANC and he did it. In 1961 they asked him to ban the NDP and he did it. . . . In 1962 they asked him to ban the ZAPU and he did it. . . . The European minority, led by Sir Edgar, is the real enemy of law and order since they do not want the vote to be extended to 4,000,000 Africans in Southern Rhodesia.[13]

ZAPU was beginning to realize that there was little hope for change by constitutional means and began increasingly

[12] Davis M'Gabe, in *Africa Report,* Feb. 1967, p. 19.

[13] Mimeographed, mass-circulation letter.

to resort to means previously considered unconstitutional. Furthermore, ZAPU was evolving an ideology based on the legitimacy of their cause (on their disadvantageous position) rather than on the future reconstruction of society.

## *Conflict between ZAPU and ZANU*

Shortly after the banning of ZAPU a new development took place in African nationalist politics. In 1963, because of pressures within Rhodesia, Nkomo decided that a government-in-exile would be able to achieve more, especially in the international sphere, and so he decided to move the ZAPU executive to Dar-es-Salaam. This move away from Rhodesia antagonized some members of the party executive who felt that the main struggle should be in Rhodesia. Tangible indications of tensions within ZAPU appeared in July when leaflets were circulated in Highfield suggesting the need for a new party, despite the fact that an enthusiastic Nkomo had recently said that majority rule was "just around the corner." [14] Nkomo received concrete evidence of a possible split when he obtained copies of letters Eddison Zvobgo (at that time a member of ZAPU, later on the executive of ZANU) was carrying from Dar-es-Salaam to Rhodesia.[15] At a mass meeting in Salisbury, he exposed the "rebels"—Sithole, Takawira, Morton Malianga, and Mugabe—and subsequently dismissed them from the party. J. Z. Moyo, Joseph Msika, and Clement Muchache stayed with ZAPU. Among others dismissed by Nkomo were Enos Nkala and Stanley Pari-

[14] *African Daily News,* June 24, 1963.
[15] Shamuyarira, *Crisis in Rhodesia,* p. 181.

rewa, who had not gone to Dar-es-Salaam. It is debatable whether Sithole planned to oust Nkomo from ZAPU and take over the leadership of the party or whether the circumstances surrounding his dismissal forced him to found a new party. One thing is clear: Nkomo was unwilling to countenance any dissent within ZAPU.

Sithole returned to Rhodesia and, with the blessing of President Julius Nyerere of Tanganyika, established a new nationalist party. The Zimbabwe African National Union (ZANU) charged Nkomo with circumvention and indecisiveness: "ZANU was formed last August after it had been realized that through weak, insincere and cowardly leadership the struggle of the oppressed people of Zimbabwe had faltered and was strenuously grinding to a halt." [16] Because many ZANU supporters were Shonas (the party operated out of the Shona stronghold of Salisbury) and Nkomo and many of his followers were Ndebeles, a possible ethnic reason for the split has often been implied.[17] While it cannot be denied that ethnic tension existed in Rhodesia as a result of different cultural and language backgrounds and because of the nineteenth-century Ndebele conquest of the Shona, widespread socialization into a modern, urban-based society had cut into the differences. While friction had periodically occurred between the two groups, intermarriage had also taken place. As Herbert L. Spiro maintains, "The issue has so

[16] *Zimbabwe To-Day,* 1, no. 1 (Feb. 1964), 1.

[17] Sithole's father was born in Gazaland where the Shangaan (Ndua), an early Zulu immigratory group, had settled and intermarried with the Shona. His mother was a Ndebele. He was, thus, in the interesting position of speaking both languages and understanding both cultures.

far been raised only in relatively unimportant contexts."[18]

Efforts were made within the nationalist parties to transcend such divisions. Nkomo and Sithole and many other Ndebeles and Shonas had worked together in the ANC, the NDP, and ZAPU. The split between ZAPU and ZANU was based on Nkomo's leadership rather than his Ndebele background, but tensions with an ethnic basis have continued[19]—in April 1970, for example, a "running battle" took place in Lusaka between Shona and Ndebele supporters of ZAPU.

The white government actively encouraged the view that ethnic ferment existed and that the white presence in Rhodesia prevented bloodshed. ZANU maintained that it stood for democratic rule and that its character was nonracial, although it did believe in a predominantly African character for independent Rhodesia, which would be renamed Zimbabwe. In a policy statement ZANU claimed that it represented the "fighting spirit which began with an imposed rule in 1890. We have a duty to ourselves and to the unborn generations of Zimbabwe, and the duty is to free Zimbabwe. We are our own liberators."[20] ZANU's aims included the establishment of a nationalist, democratic, socialist, and Pan-Africanist republic; adult suffrage; rule of law and separation of powers; European immigration of technicians and investors only, excluding whites from South Africa and the Portuguese Territories; repeal of all color discrimination and repressive laws; entrenchment

18 Herbert L. Spiro, "The Rhodesias and Nyasaland," in *Five African States: Responses to Diversity,* Gwendolen M. Carter, ed. (Ithaca: Cornell University Press, 1963), p. 391.

19 See *Africa Research Bulletin,* Jan. 1–31, 1971, p. 1964.

20 Ndabaningi Sithole, mimeographed letter.

of a bill of rights in the constitution; all land under national control with the government as the people's trustee; amnesty for all political prisoners; free health service and unemployment relief; compulsory secondary education to the level of form 2.

As indicated by its choice of officers, ZANU attracted African intellectuals; it aimed at a vertically supported movement—"a grass roots alliance organization of peasants, peasant farmers, businessmen, students, the chiefs and headmen and the professional men and women." [21] Nkomo, nevertheless, still retained mass support because of his remarkable ability on the one level to reorganize ZAPU (the permanent staff of ZAPU remained loyal to him), and on the other to draw large crowds of followers. The extent of this support was underestimated by expatriate members of ZAPU and by many operating within Rhodesia itself. While Nkomo's leadership left a great deal to be desired on a day-to-day organizational level, he had considerable ability to generate mass support and approval.

Several members of ZAPU were concerned about the split because they felt that African unity was vital if sustained opposition against the white power structure was to be maintained. They would have preferred to have competition for leadership emerge and be resolved within ZAPU.

It is of interest to note that the ZAPU-ZANU split was the first major ideological and structural division in African nationalist politics in Southern Rhodesia. In the past, African politics were characterized by division between the traditional and the modern, the rural and the urban. However, the polarization of nationalist politics by the

[21] *Battle Cry,* March 27, 1964.

establishment of two distinct organizations was an entirely new variable. Because many of the leaders of the new organization had in the past been part of the Youth League, the ANC, and the NDP, there were further complications; Sithole and others in ZANU were well aware of the personal strengths and weaknesses of many of their former colleagues.

ZANU never really developed the mass support of ZAPU. It had a strong intellectual orientation and was more concerned with policy statements and ideological commitments than with structural problems; it did not have the resources that had been developed over time by previous nationalist organizations, and which ZAPU inherited.

Immediately following the split, James Chikerema rallied support for ZAPU with mass meetings and other activities. This threat to Joshua Nkomo's leadership made him aware of the need to devote himself fully to ZAPU activities. It cannot be denied that there were instances of intimidation of ZANU followers by ZAPU officials, but this point should not be overemphasized in explaining ZAPU's success with the masses. Such an explanation ignores the practical and tangible dimensions of ZAPU's leadership and organization. ZANU was too new to have sufficient resources of money and organization, nor was it prepared for Nkomo's vigorous condemnation. The choice of Ndabaningi Sithole as leader of ZANU was not a particularly wise one; at the time of the split he, too, was outside of Rhodesia, and, more importantly, he differed little from Nkomo. He certainly was not a radical to whom the extreme left wing of ZAPU might have solidly rallied. It is not surprising, therefore, that while ZAPU had little difficulty in attracting mass rallies of several thousand participants, ZANU crowds usually numbered in the hundreds; ZAPU remained the people's party.

On the day following the establishment of ZANU, Nkomo announced at Cold Comfort Farm, Salisbury, that the People's Caretaker Council (PCC) had been formed as an executive to hold the leadership of ZAPU together.[22] It was not a new and different party.

> It is a known thing to all who have been following the struggle of the African people in Southern Rhodesia that when the earlier parties were banned, i.e., African National Congress, National Democratic Party and the Zimbabwe African Peoples Union, property and moneys were taken by the Settler minority government.
>
> "Algerians decided to do without a legal political party after the French had continually banned their parties and in the end they won their independence," Nkomo said. "We cannot enjoy the luxury of political opposition at this juncture. The people must form a united front to fight against colonialism and imperialism." [23]

Other decisions made at Cold Comfort Farm were to center the struggle in Rhodesia, rather than to rely heavily upon outside intervention, and to make demands on Britain for a speedy transfer of power to the African majority.

The first sign that the dispute between the Nationalists might lead to violence had been on July 15, 1963, when

[22] From September 1957 to February 1959, the group was known as the ANC; from June 1960 to September 1961, as NDP; from December 1961 to September 1962, as ZAPU; from August 1963 to August 1964, as PCC. The term ZAPU has been used more frequently for the organization, even in 1964, than PCC.

[23] *Sunday Mail* (Salisbury), Aug. 4, 1963.

fighting took place between opposing factions of ZAPU outside Salisbury airport while members of the party were waiting for the arrival of Sithole from Tanganyika. Sithole, however, did not return to Rhodesia until July 28, and on August 9 he announced the formation of ZANU. While he was uncertain of the exact amount of support he would obtain, Sithole felt assured that at least a number of ZAPU members would go with him.

The conflict between Nkomo and Sithole was fanned by accusations and counteraccusations. Sithole referred to Nkomo as a "bully and a coward who has attempted to rule by intimidation. He loves to go from capital to capital; he loves to fly and fly and fly and in times of trouble he flies away." [24] Differences hardened, and in September 1963, Nkomo commented: "As far as I am concerned there is no question of patching it up with Sithole. He has committed political suicide." [25] The differences between the leaders were reflected by others; *Battle Cry,* the ZANU publication, aggravated the division:

A number of PCC puppet leaders, including Mr. and Mrs. Chinamano, Messrs. Enoch Dumbutshena, Wakatama, Savanhu and Joseph Msika and a group of thugs imported from Highfield were shamefully chased from the Salisbury University College by the strong ZANU university students. . . . the culprits were chased away like dogs before they even uttered a word and had to bolt away from the University grounds faster than they had come in. The students sang ZANU songs as they chased the revisionists. Only last week, Mr. Robert Mugabe, Secretary General of ZANU, had successfully addressed a meeting of the students there. Ninety-nine percent of the African students at the College are ZANU.[26]

[24] *Ibid.* [25] *Rhodesia Herald,* Sept. 14, 1963.
[26] *Battle Cry,* March 27, 1964.

## *The Rhodesian Front Responds to the Nationalists*

In February 1963 the new Rhodesian Front government had introduced what was popularly referred to as the "hanging bill," an amendment to the Law and Order (Maintenance) Act which introduced, among other things, a mandatory death sentence for types of sabotage.[27] This measure remained in force until September 1968. In addition, the Unlawful Organizations Act was amended to include the following provisions:

3. (2) If the Governor is of the opinion that an organization (a) is the parent organization of an unlawful organization; or (b) is derived from the same parent organization as an unlawful organization; or (c) is the successor of an unlawful organization; or (d) is composed substantially throughout necessarily predominantly of, or directed or controlled, directly or indirectly, by, persons who have been or are office bearers or officers of an unlawful organization; the Governor may by

[27] "37. (1) Any person who, without lawful excuse, the proof whereof lies on him, (a) by the use of petrol, benzene, benzine, parafine, methylated spirits or other inflammable liquid sets or attempts to set on fire any person, building, structure, vehicle, vessel, aircraft or railway engine, tender, carriage, van or truck; or (b) by the use of explosives (i) causes or attempts to cause injury to any person; or (ii) destroys or causes or attempts to cause damage to any building, structure, vehicle, vessel, aircraft or railway engine, tender, carriage, van or truck; shall be guilty of an offence and (c) shall be sentenced to death where such offence was committed against any person or in respect of (i) any building or structure used for residential purposes and not owned, occupied or leased by the person convicted of the offence, whether or not at the time of the commission of the offence any person was present in such building or structure" (Southern Rhodesia, *The Law and Order (Maintenance) Act* [Salisbury: Government Printer, 1959, Amended 1963], ch. 39, pp. 533–534).

proclamation in the *Gazette* declare such first mentioned organization to be an unlawful organization.[28]

The government also decided to work through the courts against the Nationalists, by bringing judicial charges against them, rather than using detention or restriction provisions. The restriction orders on the leaders of ZAPU and those that were still in force against some of the former ANC leaders were lifted, but the ban on ZAPU as a party remained in force.

Toward the end of 1963 considerable discontent was evident in the urban areas because of the presence of an overtly racist government, uncertainties surrounding the possibility of UDI, and the limited facilities for African secondary education. Both ZANU and ZAPU nurtured this discontent. They attacked schoolteachers, boycotted schools, and intimidated those who wished to attend school or to teach. Government property was destroyed in both urban and rural areas. In addition, the violence continued between ZANU and ZAPU.

In November 1963 the government banned Nkomo from attending all meetings for three months and the People's Caretaker Council from organizing any meetings for the same period. In February 1964 more than a hundred Nationalists were restricted to the isolated area of Wha Wha. The government thus moved away from its decision to operate through the courts. In March, the Law and Order (Maintenance) Act was amended to extend restriction without trial from ninety days to one year, and also to give wider discretionary powers to the police. In April, shortly after Ian Smith became prime minister, Nkomo, Msika,

[28] Southern Rhodesia, *The Unlawful Organizations Act* (Salisbury: Government Printer, 1959), ch. 81, p. 227.

and Josiah Chinamano of the PCC executive were restricted to the remote area of Gonakudzingwa and thus cut off from their followers and from active politics. Other leaders of both the PCC and ZANU were to follow Nkomo into restriction or detention. This was another step in a calculated attempt by the RF government to counteract the Nationalists. Considerable violence resulted from Nkomo's restriction, particularly in Salisbury and Bulawayo; this was spasmodic and unorganized and was aimed primarily against Africans. On August 26, 1964, ZANU, the PCC and *The African Daily News* (which was considered a pronationalist newspaper) were all banned, and a state of emergency was declared in the African suburb of Highfield, Salisbury.

*Extrasystem Operations*

From this point on, nationalist activities were directed toward overthrowing the system by unconstitutional means such as sabotage and terrorism. In a statement on August 30, 1967, the Rhodesian government recognized the full implications of the predicament: "Leaders of the two banned Rhodesian African nationalist organizations, the Zimbabwe African People's Union (ZAPU) and the Zimbabwe African National Union (ZANU), are now firmly established in Zambia, and it is from Lusaka that these people plan subversive operations directed against the Government of Rhodesia, including the infiltration of armed terrorists and offensive materials into this country." [29]

[29] Rhodesia, *Terrorist Incursions from Zambia: A Statement by The Prime Minister, The Honourable I. D. Smith* (Salisbury: Government Printer, 1967), p. 11.

Lusaka became a base for both the PCC and ZANU from which to direct sabotage and guerrilla activities, to beam propaganda broadcasts in English and the two African vernaculars, and for the printing of their various publications. Guerrilla activities involving ZAPU and the ANC of South Africa reached a high point in August 1967 in the Wankie area of Rhodesia. However, the Nationalists abandoned hopes of quick success for two reasons: they were met with strong retaliation from the Rhodesian military, which was reinforced by the South African police and military; and they suffered heavy casualties (more than a hundred were killed in the first eight months of 1968).[30] Moreover, both ZAPU and ZANU experienced difficulties in obtaining recruits. On October 15, 1969, the Zambian minister of home affairs confirmed that fifty-two Rhodesians of both ZANU and ZAPU had been arrested and then expelled to Tanzania in connection with recent kidnappings of fellow Rhodesians in Zambia for training as guerrillas.[31] The Rhodesian government responded to the guerrillas by escalating penalities for such activities and by carrying out mandatory death sentences. For example, in November 1967 the Law and Order (Maintenance) Act was extended yet again to include a mandatory death sentence "for any saboteur convicted of entering Rhodesia in possession of arms with intent to endanger the maintenance of law and order." [32]

### *The Nationalists, 1920–1974*

Whether the African Nationalists in Rhodesia attempted to utilize constitutional channels of opposition, civil dis-

[30] *African Times,* Aug. 21, 1968. [31] *Africa Report,* Jan. 1969.
[32] *Law and Order (Maintenance) Act,* as amended (1967).

obedience, international pressure, or violence, their activities have on the whole been characterized by a low level of success. How do the Rhodesian Nationalists differ from their counterparts in other parts of Africa, and, more specifically, from the successful movements in Northern Rhodesia and Nyasaland?

In an attempt to analyze their ineffectiveness, it is necessary, at the outset, to draw the distinction between domestic and historic colonialism. Domestic colonialism implies the presence of the colonial power within the boundaries of a particular country, while historic colonialism indicates an overseas power. The white population of Rhodesia may be seen as a domestic colonial power,[33] indeed one which is itself engaged in seeking independence from a historical power, Great Britain. The overthrow of an internal colonial presence poses particularly difficult problems; the power structure has a greater commitment to the maintenance of the status quo, it is in an entrenched position, and it has a wider sphere of influence.

Since it seemed hopeless to combat such a power by constitutional means, ZAPU decided to move outside of the Rhodesian system: "The repressive laws of Southern Rhodesia have ensured that no revolutionary nationalist movement can function within the country," wrote ZAPU's paper.

> If a new political party were to function, it must of necessity be a watered down and a poorer carbon copy of ZAPU. Any

[33] The Rhodesian administrative and technical services were also difficult for Africans to penetrate or undermine because of their strength and efficiency and because of white cohesion. White solidarity also meant that there was widespread unwillingness to supply arms, information, or materials to African opponents of the system.

"constitutional" means of gaining the African's lost heritage in Southern Rhodesia have dwindled with the passing of time. Through bitter lessons emphasized by time, the people of Southern Rhodesia know their only hope is through a revolutionary underground movement which will have to subvert the white supremacist regime of Southern Rhodesia before they harbour hopes of functioning normally within the boundaries of the country.[34]

This involvement clearly shows the progesssion in Rhodesian nationalist politics from system politics to a revolutionary conflict situation because of the hopelessness of operating through constitutional channels.

The Nationalists have lacked solid bases of urban and rural support, either because of the lessening of rural discontent by the government or because of the limited scope of urban organization. There has been spasmodic horizontal support from both sectors, but no sustained support which continued over time or strongly united these disparate elements. ZAPU primarily received its support from the urban masses,[35] and ZANU was an elitist party also within the urban context. There have been attitudes of protest, moments of defiance, sometimes sustained defiance, but each time the people have lapsed back into acquiescence.[36]

The Rhodesian socialization process is a partial explanation for this phenomenon. As a result of education in either mission or government schools and frequent adjustments on so many overt and subtle levels to white norms,

[34] *Zimbabwe Review,* 2, no. 1 (Aug–Sept. 1963).

[35] At its peak, ZAPU made the exaggerated claim of 175,000 members.

[36] Shamuyarira, *Crisis in Rhodesia,* p. 40.

many Africans react ambiguously to the power structure, at one and the same time seeking its approval and removal. "One of the most puzzling features of the present situation is the almost complete passivity of the African population," wrote *Black and White* in June 1967. "They seem unable to act for themselves either with violence or with non-violence. . . . And one asks oneself whether tyranny or paternalism or a combination of both have brought this about. . . . In Rhodesia to-day, we are accustomed to apparent contradiction: the astonishing unwillingness of the African to bear a grudge in spite of inhuman treatment." [37]

The internal tensions between ZAPU and ZANU dulled their thrust both internationally and within Rhodesia. There were several efforts to bring about a reconciliation, but all of these failed. For example, in 1964 the foreign ministers of Tanganyika and Zambia tried to bring the two groups together in Lusaka, but James Chikerema of ZAPU refused to sit at the same table with the ZANU representatives. In October 1965, Prime Minister Harold Wilson suggested to the leaders that a united nationalist front would be of the greatest importance—also to no avail.[38]

The Nationalists' emphasis on Great Britain and the United Nations often drew attention away from the central struggle within the country itself. In December 1970, James Chikerema, acting chairman of ZAPU, announced that he had been asked by Joshua Nkomo to start

[37] *Black and White,* June, 1967.

[38] The summit meeting held in December 1974 in Lusaka might finally have brought ZANU and ZAPU together.

negotiating with Herbert Chitepo of ZANU.[39] Immediately following this announcement, however, George Silundika, also a member of the ZAPU executive, issued a statement claiming that Nkomo had said no such thing. Silundika claimed that a united front was not in keeping with "the sociological conditions" in Zimbabwe. *The Zimbabwe News* summed up the position by stating, "Given the gravity of the situation in our country today, anyone who really knows Sithole and Nkomo would never assume that either man would idly watch the country go to the dogs in the interests of preserving the names of ZAPU and ZANU"; "militants" were merely concerned about preserving their titles in the hope that "they will one day earn ministerial posts in Salisbury." Despite Silundika's objections, a meeting did take place in January 1971 in Dar-es-Salaam between Chikerema and Chitepo under the auspices of the Liberation Committee of the Organization of African Unity, but nothing conclusive developed until the Joint Military Command in 1972.

Another effort at unity was made in 1971 with the creation of a new organization, FROLIZI (Front for the Liberation of Zimbabwe). The preamble of the draft constitution of the organization maintained that FROLIZI was formed for the purpose of uniting ZANU and ZAPU; that FROLIZI sought to bring together all people of Zimbabwe and aimed at establishing an independent, self-reliant socialist economy. The constitution also established a Revolutionary Command Council (RCC) which was described as the executive arm of the organization responsible for implementing the policies of the Central Committee.

[39] *Africa Research Bulletin,* Jan. 1–31, 1971, p. 1964.

FROLIZI was headed first by Shelton Siwela and then by James Chikerema. George Nyandoro was its executive secretary, and other members of the executive included Nelson Samkange and Nathan Shamuyarira.

In the first few months of 1973 guerrillas made considerable impact in northeastern Rhodesia, particularly in the Centenary District. At first it was not clear whether ZANU and ZAPU were cooperating or whether ZANU operated alone in the area. As time went on, it became increasingly apparent that ZANU had established links with FRELIMO (Front for the Liberation of Mozambique). The combination of these two organizations led to the most sustained and serious guerrilla attacks that white Rhodesians had to contend with. The Umtali-Beira road and the railway line became important targets. Within Rhodesia, ZANU guerrillas attempted to recruit among the Shona living in the area, secreted arms, and raided isolated farmhouses. The ZANU guerrillas were led by commanders trained in China and North Vietnam. A new generation of Africans seemed to be involved in the guerrilla activities: a group less concerned with achieving white norms and more concerned with ideology and the liberation of Rhodesia. In many ways they shared little with the older members of ZANU. The unification of ZANU and FRELIMO was countered in turn by joint Rhodesian, South African, and Portuguese retaliation. The changes in Portugese policy following the April 1974 *coup d'état* and the possibility of FRELIMO establishing the first African government of an independent Mozambique indicate considerable future support for ZANU's cause.

African nationalism has moved from political opposition—or a difference over policy goals but a willingness to operate within the system—to a conflict situation of opposition of principle in which the continued existence of the system has been challenged by means that had previously been considered illegitimate or unconstitutional. High stakes came to be involved, and the only apparent solutions were mutually incompatible. The development from voluntary association to political party and finally to extra-system operation occurred as a result of patterns of interaction between two developing nationalisms—white and African.

CHAPTER 8

# The African National Council

The African National Council (ANC) was formed in 1971 to mobilize African opposition to the proposals of the Pearce Commission. Specifically, the ANC wanted Africans to realize the power of unity and to "move as one people" toward achieving freedom. It intended to explain and expose the "dangerous implications" of acceptance of the settlement proposals and to raise funds for the promotion of the ANC, "a temporary body to execute the task before us."[1] Its leader, Bishop Abel Muzorewa, maintained that negotiations leading to the constitutional proposals, either between Sir Alec Douglas-Home and the British government or with Lord Goodman, had not included Africans, and that Great Britain was now merely consulting African opinion in order to give some form of respectability to an already concluded deal.[2]

Bishop Muzorewa perceived the founding of the organization as a result of spontaneous African concern in both the urban and rural areas following the publication of the White Paper on the Pearce Commission. This was a new direction in African political organization: a response to deep-rooted African concerns rather than an effort to gen-

[1] *Africa Research Bulletin,* Dec. 1–31, 1971.

[2] Bishop Muzorewa had been head of the United Methodist Church in Rhodesia; he was born in 1925. The vice-president of the ANC was the Reverend Canaan Banana, born in 1936.

erate political activity or to educate the African public in order to elicit a response. He saw the threat of an independent Rhodesia under white control as a matter of overriding concern to all Africans. "At home we have long forgotten the ZANU-ZAPU conflict. The National Executive of ANC has people from both groups and people who have never been in any party." [3]

The primary thrust, according to the bishop, was to organize strong opposition to the Pearce Commission. "The Constitutional provisions are so full of reservations and escape clauses, the declaration of rights are so open to abuse, as to render the document meaningless. For every right there is a restriction which renders it void. The road to majority rule is boobytrapped every inch of the way." [4] The organizeis planned to campaign in both urban and rural areas, and as early as December 1971 they had established branch organizations in Epworth and Mrewa.

The ANC gave early indication that it was considerably to the left of existing African constitutional political parties. Its active participants included several prominent African Nationalists such as Eddison Zvobgo, formerly a member of ZANU; [5] Edson Sithole, formerly a member of the ZANU executive; Josiah Chinamano, a former member of the ZAPU executive and a close adviser of Nkomo; and Michael Mawema and Simon Moyo, former members of ZANU.[6] The choice of the name African National

[3] *Times* (London), Feb. 8, 1972.

[4] *Manchester Guardian,* March 9, 1972.

[5] Zvobgo had been in prison in Salisbury for seven years with no trial.

[6] Linkages with ZANU were (and have clearly remained) strong. There had been no public statement to this effect, but even a superficial review of membership and policies clearly indicated this.

Council, and in particular the abbreviation "ANC," had obvious significance. The organizers intended it to act as a reminder of the long tradition of African nationalist politics, and specifically the African National Congress. In many ways the ANC of the 1950's was an important mass movement, and the resurrection of this acronym was indicative of a conscious effort to recall the successful and unified days before the split between ZANU and ZAPU.

The stated aims of the ANC included rejection of a settlement with Great Britain on the proposed terms; attempts to fuse the two former nationalist organizations; attempts to operate in both the rural and urban areas; efforts to obtain African trade union support; and support of the African Christian churches.

In his evidence to the Pearce Commission, Bishop Muzorewa stated, "This is the first and last chance for the African people to pass a verdict on white minority rule. Our rejection of the proposals is unanimous." [7] The Bishop rejected the proposals because they entrenched and perpetuated white racism, and implementation might lead to revolution.

Michael Mawema, organizing secretary of the African National Council, told the commission, "Our freedom is not guaranteed a half hour after you have left. . . . We are sacrificing our own freedom by appearing before you. When you have gone we will probably not be heard of any more." [8]

Eddison Zvobgo, deputy secretary general of the ANC,

[7] Great Britain Cmnd. 4964 (1972), *Rhodesia: Report of the Commission on Rhodesian Opinion under the Chairmanship of the Right Honourable Lord Pearce,* p. 122.

[8] *Washington Post,* Jan. 29, 1972.

said if Africans accepted the proposals they "would be the only species of human being who ever went down on record as saying, yes, it's nice to be ruled by a minority in your own land." [9]

The African National Council leaders were opposed to the spurious character of the franchise proposals. To qualify for the African higher voters' roll an African voter would need a high school education and a monthly income of $200 [10] or other property qualifications. When the roll reached 6 per cent of the number of registered white voters, two new seats for blacks would be added to Parliament (fifty white and sixteen blacks held seats at the time) and each time another 6 per cent advance was achieved two more seats would be added. Edson Sithole, publicity chairman of the ANC, told Lord Pearce that he estimated that the number of additional blacks who would qualify each year would be about 300 to 400 at the most.[11]

The emergence of the African National Council, and its overwhelming rejection of the settlement proposals to the Pearce Commission, must be seen as a significant milestone in African political involvement. The formation of the ANC indicated strong vertical support from all classes and all sectors of the African community. The last major African Nationalist political engagement had taken place in 1961–1962, when African national leaders opposed the Whitehead constitution. In the following ten years nationalist politics had been characterized by the split and dissension between ZANU and ZAPU and by overwhelm-

[9] *New York Times,* Jan. 19, 1972.

[10] In Rhodesian dollars. One Rhodesian dollar is equal to 90 U.S. cents.

[11] *New York Times,* Jan. 19, 1972.

ing difficulties in attempting to organize a resistance struggle from outside of Rhodesia; the entrenched position of the Smith regime had stifled any form of internal nationalist activity.

The intervening ten years had also resulted in the solidarity of white Rhodesians behind the RF and Smith, fewer contacts between the races, and decreased possibilities for African constitutional political participation.

The original decision to implement the proposal was based on the expectation, by both the British government and Ian Smith, that the African opposition to the settlement would be moderate. This expectation proved quite wrong. In the urban areas mass demonstrations broke out and several Africans were killed, while in the rural areas—Tribal Trust Lands where the African National Council was not permitted to operate and where chiefs were essentially paid civil servants of the government—there was also strong disapproval.

The former federal prime minister, Sir Roy Welensky, said, "the grass had to be dry enough to burn. If this thing is turned down it will have been turned down because there is no trust of the government by the Africans." [12] Indeed, Sir Roy Welensky went so far as to say that he felt that for the first time Africa had a veto over the future of Rhodesia.[13]

Desmond Lardner-Burke, the minister of justice and law and order, epitomized the Smith government's lack of understanding of the African position: "If the British had lived up to an agreement to test African opinion immediately after signing of the proposed settlement in Novem-

12 *Financial Times* (London), June 2, 1972.
13 *Washington Post,* Jan. 29, 1972.

ber, militant dissonance would not have had a chance to organize opposition and riots would not have occurred."[14]

Perhaps the most important dimension of the African response to the Pearce Commission was the recognition by African leaders that they were now an important and active political force in Rhodesia. Bishop Muzorewa maintained that this was the first time in ten years that Africans had actively participated in the Rhodesian political process. An important finding of the commission was that Rhodesia, far from being a country of placid politics, was in fact "alive with political activity at the grass roots."[15]

In addition, the Rhodesian government also underestimated the seven African M.P.'s of the Rhodesian Electoral Union who, in a memorandum to the Pearce Commission, formally rejected the settlement terms. The government had also miscalculated the "loyalty" of the tribal M.P.'s.

The general approach among most white Rhodesians (and especially those in official capacities) since UDI had been that Rhodesia could not afford any form of opposition. Consequently, any reports from district commissioners and others indicating African discontent were frowned upon. But, while the extent and virulence of African opposition apparently came as a surprise to many white Rhodesians, the surprise in fact should have been that it was not more extensive.

As a result of the "no" vote on the settlement proposal, the 1969 constitution remained in force in Rhodesia. Unlike the changes proposed, it provided for vague parity in the far distant future. It was not the aim of the African leaders to continue to operate under this constitution;

[14] *Ibid.* [15] *Report of the Pearce Commission*, p. 37.

their emphasis on a "no" vote was aimed at keeping a settlement from being reached, or, as Bishop Muzorewa maintained at a press conference at the United Nations on February 16, 1972, "to avoid the legalization of UDI which would have resulted in the re-colonization rather than the de-colonization of Rhodesia." [16]

The achievement of this goal did not result in an end to white control of the political process. The ANC appeared somewhat bewildered, not by its success, but about where to go from there. If indeed it had a veto, it had one only when Britain participated in political negotiations, not in day-to-day Rhodesian politics. African dissatisfaction in 1972 must not be seen in the same terms as the campaigns of 1961–1962. Discontent was much deeper and much more widespread. The vertical African involvement of former Nationalists, chiefs, and others was indicative of greater impatience with the system than ever before. The intervention of the Pearce Commission had presented the opportunity for many to express dissatisfaction to an outside agency.

Within this context, the ANC leaders' next move was to propose a national convention. The plan outlined by Bishop Muzorewa was obviously intended for British government consideration since it was unrealistic in terms of Rhodesian politics. The four-stage plan called for a convention in which representatives of all political parties would participate. In addition there would be representatives of the churches, business communities, trade unions, civil servants, local authorities, and so on. The aim of the convention would be to "examine the desirability of a settlement and the convening of a constitutional confer-

[16] *Africa Digest,* April 1972, p. 28.

erence." [17] The plan also envisioned observers from both the U.N. and the Organization of African Unity. Not unexpectedly, Ian Smith immediately rejected the idea of such a convention on the grounds that his government did not recognize the ANC's right to speak for Africans.

Bishop Muzorewa's central message was a reminder to the British government that because Africans did not participate in the initial talks between the Rhodesian and British governments, the proposals tested by the Pearce Commission failed. If Britain were once more to engage in constitutional discussions it could not do so on a unilateral basis with white Rhodesian politicians. The scope of future discussion was then elaborated upon by the ANC.

## *The ANC and Party Structure*

In March, members of the executive of the ANC announced that they were forming a new political-action group to carry on the struggle against white minority rule.[18] Josiah Gondo, the only member of the National People's Union in the Rhodesian Parliament, announced the dissolution of the NPU and urged members to join the ANC.[19] A party manifesto issued by Bishop Muzorewa stated, "We shall not deviate from our just demand for universal adult suffrage." Bishop Muzorewa said that the

[17] *Financial Times,* June 2, 1972.

[18] The ANC executive was made up of Bishop Abel T. Muzorewa (president), Rev. Canaan Banana (vice-president), Carlton C. Ngcebetsha (secretary general), Rev. Henry Kachidza (treasurer general), Edson F. C. Sithole (publicity secretary), Arthur Chadzingwa (barrister-at-law, organizing secretary), Mrs. Tanjiwe Lesabe (secretary for women), Mrs. L. Kutama (deputy secretary for women), A. Ndabambi (secretary for external affairs), R. T. D. Sadomba, M.P. (deputy secretary for external affairs).

[19] *Rhodesia Herald,* March 10, 1972.

organizers would attempt to work toward a constitutional conference at which representatives of black and white Rhodesia and Great Britain would negotiate "a just settlement." While the manifesto stated that the ANC believed in the "invincibility of numbers," Bishop Muzorewa nevertheless emphasized a nonviolent approach in which civil disobedience would be acceptable.[20] Indeed, the Bishop, in the face of a "no" vote from the Pearce Commission, was still trying to keep constitutional channels open. He felt that it would be "blindsightedness" for Britain and Rhodesia to refuse any group which wanted to display responsibility and cooperation on a constitutional level because the alternative to this would be a return to underground activities.

The ANC had clearly moved from being a pressure group to what it now referred to as "an organization." It was not terming itself a political party, however. The organizers established a national executive of fifty-five members (twenty-three of whom were to serve on the central committee). Many of these had been part of former nationalist organizations. In addition, it organized a "national assembly" of 140 persons to be elected by members of the organization. This national assembly was to be "not a parliament of Rhodesia, but a mere organ of the ANC." [21] The ANC once again emphasized its linkages with previous nationalist activity. The group maintained that it was the "heir to the people's struggle which had ceaselessly been waged since the imposition of alien rule in 1890." [22] Furthermore, while the manifesto stated that the rights and property of whites should be protected, the ANC did not

[20] *New York Times,* March 11, 1972. [21] *Ibid.*
[22] *Africa Research Bulletin,* March 1–31, 1972.

believe "in the minorities' amassing of social, political and economic privileges at the expense of the freedom of the majority." [23]

The ANC was prevented from issuing membership cards by the Rhodesian government, which claimed that such cards would become weapons of intimidation.[24] In June the *Government Gazette* declared the ANC a "designated" political party and prevented it from obtaining funds from foreign sources under the emergency powers (prohibition of foreign aid to designated political parties, regulation 1972). Specifically, the minister of justice and law and order, Desmond Lardner-Burke, maintained that the ANC had "been responsible for actions interefering with the peace, order and good government of Rhodesia and the receipt of external assistance to the ANC would be likely to interfere with public safety, the maintenance of public order, and the preservation of peace." [25]

The Rhodesian government was clearly fearful of banning the organization because to do so at that stage would have closed the door to the even remote possibility of future talks. With the grasp of power out of its reach the ANC itself had already begun to suffer from internal ideological differences between those who wanted to work within the system when immediate rewards were not forthcoming and those who wanted more radical action. The ANC may be seen as yet another manifestation of system political participation. The fact that its leaders had considered backing candidates for the sixteen African seats and for the local councils in the Tribal Trust Lands indi-

[23] *New York Times,* March 11, 1972.
[24] *Rhodesia Herald,* March 27, 1972.
[25] *Star* (Johannesburg), June 10, 1972.

cated a willingness to operate within the system. While Bishop Muzorewa was determined to continue an internal constitutional struggle, Eddison Zvobgo and others chose to resign from the ANC.

In March and April of 1973, Ian Smith and Bishop Muzorewa met and discussed possible terms for a settlement. The very fact of their entering a dialogue indicates the ANC's clear willingness to operate on a constitutional level.[26] Smith was aware that agreement with the ANC was the key to ending the constitutional impasse and that in fact this was the only African group willing to enter negotiations with him which had credibility with Britain. Despite the urgency of reaching agreement, Smith found the ANC's terms unacceptable. In a statement in the House of Assembly he listed ANC demands: immediate parity for African and white members of Parliament; the release and the granting of amnesty to all held in detention or engaged in guerrilla activities; the repeal of the Land Tenure Act; the repeal of all discriminatory legislation; granting to Britain the right to veto certain sections of the constitution; and the broadening of the franchise.[27] For Smith this was too close to the idea of "one man–one vote" for comfort, and he maintained that the demands were totally and absolutely unacceptable. In the succeeding months, the ANC and the Smith government followed an ambiguous pattern of interaction. In July 1973 six of the ANC's top officials were detained, and further detentions were made in August. The minister of justice and law and order saw

[26] Because of the number of ZANU supporters who joined the ANC, it might have represented constitutional efforts by ZANU, counterbalanced by its guerrilla activities in northeastern Rhodesia, but there is little evidence to substantiate this view.

[27] *Rhodesia Herald,* June 30, 1973.

the ANC as a security risk and justified these actions on this basis. Nevertheless, there were indications of continued communication, and Muzorewa himself maintained that, despite the round-up of twenty ANC officials, he was still willing to enter talks with the prime minister. Despite the subsequent removal of his passport, Bishop Muzorewa was consistently willing to enter discussions with the Smith regime.

As negotiations with Bishop Muzorewa continued, Smith was willing to make only minimal concessions, even though the support of the ANC was crucial to settling the constitutional deadlock. After several months of discussions Smith offered the ANC two extra seats in the House of Assembly, thus bringing the total African representation from sixteen to eighteen seats. Edson Sithole summed up the ANC response to this proposal. "We are willing to have an interim sort of arrangement, one where the Europeans will not dominate the Africans or the Africans the Europeans—in other words some form of parity. But we won't accept less than parity." [28] Sithole went on to say that even the parity formula was a big concession on the part of the ANC and that such an arrangement would be unique on the African continent. Prior to the 1974 election Smith offered to increase African representation by a total of six additional seats but this was also found unacceptable by the ANC.[29] In addition it also stated that it would boycott the constitutional conference which Smith intended to organize. It is ironic that while Smith attempted to win the support of the ANC he simultaneously

28 *Washingon Post,* Jan. 28, 1974.

29 In the 1974 election unofficial supporters of the ANC (the organization itself did not participate) won all six seats they contested.

took action to curb the more outspoken members of the organization. Thus, by the time of the 1974 election Edson Sithole and at least fifty other ANC supporters were in detention.

CHAPTER 9

# The United People's Party: African Constitutional Opposition

Opposition is perhaps the central reality of politics; there are always those who hold and wield power and those who do not but who seek to gain power, or at least to keep a check on those who have power. In Rhodesia, white opposition parties have been little more than variations of the ruling party. But what of African opposition? Must it also be classified in these terms, or is it substantially different? Are there inherently Rhodesian limits to the scope of African opposition in Rhodesia, or do the parameters of the concept of constitutional opposition transcend the particular? By looking at the constitutional African opposition in the Rhodesian Parliament it will be possible to obtain a better perspective of the Rhodesian political system as a whole and to understand the conditions that drove the Nationalists away from constitutional politics. Above all, it should provide insights into the potentialities and limitations of constitutional political opposition in an authoritarian system.

## *The United People's Party: Genesis*

The United People's Party, the first African parliamentary opposition party in Rhodesia's history, did not emerge as the result of African demands for a party to represent their interests, nor did it arise from a firm base of popular support. Its genesis was purely circumstantial—the result of the decline in support for the Rhodesia Party, the successor of the UFP by the white electorate. In 1962 the UFP received 19,302 votes and the RF 19,289 while in 1965 the RF polled 23,381 votes and the UFP 7,854.[1]

In the 1965 election the Rhodesia Party received a substantial portion of the A-roll votes, but none of its white candidates was returned to office. The executive of the party under the leadership of David Butler felt that a parliamentary caucus could not be led from outside Parliament, and the party was, therefore, disbanded. "There seemed no certain future in trying to keep the Party intact under the leadership of one of the M.P.'s elected on the B Roll." [2]

The Rhodesia Party having gone into "cold storage," its ten African members formed themselves on May 31, 1965, into the United People's Party, which became the official opposition in the Rhodesian Parliament, under the leadership of Josiah M. Gondo, the first African to hold the position of leader of the Opposition. The party chairman was Chad M. Chipunza, a former parliamentary secretary in the Federal Parliament.

Declared one African M.P., Percy M'Kudu: "The United People's Party came into being after our European friends had been eliminated in the snap 1965 national election. This came about because some Europeans did not agree to become members of an entirely African-led opposition in Parliament, and we were forced to change our name. We choose United People's Party because it

1 *Central African Examiner,* 8, no. 11 (June 1965), 6–7.

2 *Rhodesia Herald,* June 1, 1965. The RP won ten out of fifteen seats and received a total of 754 B-roll votes.

would embrace people of all races if they felt they would like to be a united people." [3] The UPP was essentially a black version of the RP and was committed, as was its predecessor, to working within and sustaining the political system. From the outset, it expressed a willingness to operate within the parliamentary framework of the Rhodesian political system: "We want to show that we are responsible parliamentarians who are capable of advancing the constitution." [4] The UPP began to operate, then, in an institutionalized system which clearly defined legitimate means of competition. The party made it clear that it was going to be an opposition which would oppose but not obstruct.[5] It would oppose the activities and policies of the government in power but would not move beyond the defined boundaries of the political system.

The old RP, for its part, formed a new organization (rather than a political party), the Rhodesian Constitutional Association (RCA), which was "open to those who support the basic principles of racial cooperation as the only long-term solution." [6] Gondo and other members of

[3] Interview, Salisbury, Aug. 1, 1967. [4] *Ibid.*

[5] See Giovanni Sartori, "Opposition and Control: Problems and Prospects," *Government and Opposition*, 1, no. 2 (Feb. 1966), 151.

[6] *Constitution of the Rhodesian Constitutional Association* (Salisbury: RCA, 1965), p. 1. A letter from the honorary secretary of the RCA presented their version of the situation: "The last general election brought about a completely new situation in Rhodesia's political affairs. For the first time Parliament is divided racially between a white Government and a black Opposition. The Rhodesia Party found itself represented by 10 B Roll Members, but with no A Roll seats and thus it ceased to be a multi-racial party in Parliament.

"Many problems arose from this, and these were fully discussed and debated at a meeting of the Party's Central Executive. The basic belief was reaffirmed on all sides that the principle of racial cooperation provides the only long-term solution to Rhodesia's future. It the UPP parliamentary caucus agreed to be members of the RCA's national committee and to draw on the parliamentary experiences of the former opposition. In time, however, this relationship was to prove superficial. The white opposition had sensed the mood of the Rhodesian electorate and had withdrawn into itself. John Morgan, white vice-president of the UPP, commented that this withdrawal was "an absolute mistake because of the need for a really viable opposition. The whites were not prepared to carry on. They slapped the black man in the face." [7]

The suddenness with which it had come into existence meant that the UPP was a party in name only. It did not have a set of historical events to define its identity as an African party; it had no specific claims to legitimacy beyond the fact that some of its members had been part of the RP, and it had not articulated any ideological position. Indeed, it had not held a party congress and was without a constitution or even a basic statement of principles. Furthermore, patterns of authority within the party had

---

was also agreed that it would not be possible to continue the Rhodesia Party as a formal political entity in the new situation without causing embarrassment to members, both inside and outside Parliament. It was therefore agreed to suspend (not liquidate) the Party until such time as it might again be able to serve its purpose. Meanwhile the African M.P.'s formed themselves into the United People's Party, subscribing to the basic principle of racial cooperation, but giving themselves much more freedom and flexibility in day-to-day debate than would be possible if they were tied rigidly to a Rhodesia Party largely controlled from outside the House.

"At the same time those outside Parliament formed themselves into the Rhodesian Constitutional Association in order to keep alive the basic principles of racial cooperation without being bound to a policy on matters of detail" (mimeographed letter from Hon. Sec. of RCA to members of the Association, 1965).

[7] Interview, Salisbury, Aug. 20, 1967.

not been defined, and policy statements by Gondo and others were, of necessity, cautious and pragmatic.

Gondo maintained that his party opposed one man–one vote but that ultimately universal adult suffrage would have to come—by constitutional means.[8] Chad Chipunza, as party chairman, elaborated on the party's goals. He said the UPP would resist any attempts at a Unilateral Declaration of Independence, would aim at the removal of all "unnecessary forms of racial discrimination," would seek to extend the vote to as many as possible, and would work to obtain free primary education for all Rhodesians. He also maintained that the principles of the UPP were in keeping with the ideals of the Rhodesia Party but were drawn to meet the needs of an all-black opposition.[9]

Fifteen members had been elected to the Legislative Assembly on the B roll, but only ten joined the UPP when it first came into existence; the remaining five sat in the House as independents. Three of these five were Africans, one was white (perhaps the most outstanding opponent of the Rhodesian Front, Dr. Ahrn Palley, the representative for Highfield, the large African suburb of Salisbury), and the fifth was an Indian, Behaba Govan, who represented Magondi. Gondo tried to gain the parliamentary support of the independents: "The road is open for the independents to join us. The first move is up to them. We have common ideals and a common goal." [10] By November 1965, two of the independents, Isaac Samuriwo and P. E. Chigogo, had joined the UPP. A third, Patrick Rubatika, had planned to join at this time, but when members of the UPP walked out of the opening session of the Legisla-

[8] *Rhodesia Herald,* June 2, 1965.
[9] *Ibid.,* July 3, 1965.
[10] *Ibid.,* June 1, 1965.

tive Assembly following UDI, he changed his mind. He claimed that they were "foolish and irresponsible" for not recognizing the *de facto* government of Ian Smith.[11] Rubatika subsequently joined the party, however, and brought it to its full complement of thirteen members.

Why did these Africans choose to work within the Rhodesian system? Were factors such as age, education, and political socialization discernible influences in their choice? In the restricted Rhodesian social system there could be only limited variations in the backgrounds of both nationalist and constitutionally-minded politicians. They were all in the African elite because of their education, and they were all held down by the same racial barriers.[12] Most UPP and Nationalist leaders were educated in mission schools and shared more or less the same process of socialization into the white-dominated Rhodesian society. Nonetheless, there was a considerable difference in the political attitudes of the groups. The average age of the members of the UPP was 50 in 1967; thus they were about ten years older than the Nationalists, whose median age was 39. This substantiates James R. Scarrit's premise that there was a substantial generation difference between Nationalists and UPP members. Scarrit attributes the ideological difference between the groups to the different times at which individuals came onto the changing Rhodesian political scene, and also to some extent an increase in conservatism as individuals grow older.

Higher education was another important variable. None

11 *Ibid.*, Nov. 27, 1965.

12 See James R. Scarrit, "The Adoption of Political Styles by African Politicians in Rhodesia," *Midwest Journal of Political Science,* 10, no. 1 (Feb. 1966), 7.

of the members of the UPP had studied abroad; most of them did postsecondary studies in Rhodesia or South Africa. Many of the Nationalists, on the other hand, had been educated in Britain or the United States. The following members of the UPP studied in South Africa: Chad Chipunza, B.A., Fort Hare; Isaac Samuriwo, certificate in agriculture, Agricultural School, Tsolo; Patrick Rubatika, Adams Teachers College; E. J. Mhlanga, McCord Zulu Hospital, Natal; Cephas Hlbangana, Fort Hare; Percy M'Kudu, Jan Hofmeyr School of Social Science, Johannesburg. Those who continued their education in Rhodesia were Josiah Gondo, P. E. Chigogo, Luke Kandengwa, and Ranches Makaya.

The types of careers that members of the two groups engaged in were also important variables. Several of the Nationalist leaders had independent career bases such as the medical profession, law, or the trade unions. For example, Joshua Nkomo was a social worker, Ndabaningi Sithole a minister, Herbert Chitepo a barrister, and T. G. Silundika had been a university research assistant. The UPP members tended to have worked either for governmental agencies or to have been under the direct control of such agencies. Chipunza, Rubatika, Hlbangana, Makaya, and J. S. Hove were all either schoolteachers or headmasters. Chigogo served with the Rhodesian army from 1947 to 1951. Ambrose Majongwe and M'Kudu at one time worked for the British South Africa police force. Kandengwa and Mhlanga worked for the Rhodesian government as medical aides; Kandengwa subsequently went into business, establishing a successful hotel for Africans at Norton. Other businessmen were Gondo and Samuriwo.

Several members of the UPP had experience on school

boards and voluntary associations. Chad Chipunza was at one time vice-president of the Southern Rhodesian African Teachers' Association; Isaac Samuriwo was chairman of the board of the Nyatsime Training College. Patrick Rubatika founded the Southern Rhodesia African Teachers' Association in 1942 and for many years remained with the organization as its secretary. Luke Kandengwa was the the founder and chairman of St. Eric's School. Ambrose Majongwe was on the executive of the African Farmers' Union and also established and served as the president of the Catholic Association.

In terms of political socialization, only two of the members of the UPP had direct involvement with the Nationalists: Gondo had been a member of the ANC and Chigogo had been treasurer of the NDP. Chipunza had played an important role in the Capricorn Africa Society. Samuriwo's ambiguous political history included having run unsuccessfully as a candidate for the Rhodesian Front. Mhlanga had worked for the Bulawayo city council from 1941 to 1949. Kandengwa had been chairman of the Norton African Advisory Committee and had also been on the executive of the UFP. Hlbangana had been a member of the UFP, and it had been rumored that Sir Edgar Whitehead was grooming him for a cabinet-level appointment after the 1962 election. Majongwe had worked in the field of community development and was also on the Executive of the Southern Rhodesian Association, which represented the chiefs. M'Kudu had worked in the Rhodesian courts as an interpreter, for the municipality of Cape Town, South Africa, and for the municipality of Umtali as a welfare officer. Makaya had been secretary of the Bikita Native Council for more than ten years.

There is a pattern, then, of involvement in legitimate organizations and an acceptance of and operation within the prevailing system. Part of the answer to the question of political involvement is to be found by looking back to the Federation. In the period from Federation onward, Africans who wanted to participate in politics had two choices: they could either join the political parties dominated by the whites and hope to come to prominence within them, or they could join the Nationalists. There were more immediate rewards and fewer risks for those who worked within the ranks of the parties. Thus, for example, Chad Chipunza soon rose to an important position in the Federal Parliament. It is interesting to note in this respect that Joshua Nkomo, in 1954, ran for the Matabeleland seat in the Federal Parliament but lost to J. S. Hove in an election in which whites voted predominantly. Success within the system might therefore be isolated as a further variable. The members of the UPP had operated successfully in voluntary associations, quasi-political organizations, and, finally, from 1962 onward, in the House; first as members of the UFP, then of the RP, and finally of the UPP. But despite certain uniformities in their backgrounds and in their approaches to politics, the union of the African M.P.'s in the UPP was not comfortable.

### *Rivalry and Tension within the Party: The Selection of Personnel*

Josiah Gondo had become leader of the Opposition in May 1965 as a "caretaker" leader, and afterward there was considerable vying for this position within the party. The post of leader of the Opposition carried not only a considerable amount of prestige but also a special parliamentary allowance—increasing the regular M.P. salary from £2,500 ($7,000) to £3,500 ($9,800). In particular, Chad Chipunza felt that his federal experience equipped him for the position. In March 1966, after a six-hour parliamentary caucus, Chipunza was elected the new leader of the Opposition, Gondo became deputy president of the party and Isaac Samuriwo, party chairman. The UPP officially maintained that there was no change in principles, but rather that "a more dynamic approach was hoped for."[13]

In April there were further rumblings of discontent. Mhlanga voiced four overt causes: the manner in which the caucus had appointed Chipunza leader of the party; the failure of the party to call a congress; a fear that the party was in danger of losing its multiracial character; and the fact that Chipunza had not reported to the Opposition about a recent trip to Britain, where he consulted with the British government.[14] Although these were positive areas of discontent, E. J. Mhlanga and J. M. Behane, who supported him, were engaging in a power play. In order to avoid a split in the party, Mhlanga was appointed deputy chairman and Behane, deputy chief whip (Luke Kandengwa was chief whip).

Clearly, there was an urgent need for a party congress to resolve the problems of unity and leadership. The UPP issued a formal statement that Gondo had merely been appointed "caretaker" leader, that Chipunza had been accepted by the caucus, and that time was needed to build up branches in the country before calling a congress. At the same time it distributed, in a mass-circulation leaflet, the party principles: (1) To develop a happy and prosper-

[13] *Rhodesia Herald,* March 26, 1966. [14] *Ibid.,* April 23, 1966.

ous Rhodesia, in which all sections can live together in harmony, free from fear and racial prejudice; (2) to obtain independence by negotiation for Rhodesia within the Commonwealth on terms acceptable to the majority of the inhabitants of the country, and with adequate safeguards for the rights of all; (3) to resist any attempts to alter the constitution or status of Rhodesia by unlawful means;[15] (4) to revise the present system of voting rights in order to extend the vote to as many people as possible; (5) to remove all unnecessary forms of racial discrimination; (6) to maintain the standards of the civil service; (7) to provide free primary education to all Rhodesian children, together with a massive development of secondary and technical education; (8) to review the present system of local government, so as to engender a sense of belonging in every individual; (9) to promote immigration on a selective basis, to ensure that all immigrants will easily be assimilated in Rhodesia and will be able to contribute to the prosperity of the country; (10) to encourage nonpolitical trade unions; (11) to achieve stability in the country and to encourage investment and industrial development; (12) to expand production in the rural areas, through the provision of loan funds and other economic help.[16]

UPP Platform

There can be no doubt that Chad Chipunza had treated his party in a rather cavalier manner. In addition, several factors now played against him: first, in April, 1966, he suggested that a national government should be formed to face the crisis surrounding the illegal declaration of independence in Rhodesia. Mhlanga and Hlbangana immedi-

[15] This was written prior to UDI.

[16] "Principles of the United People's Party" (Fort Victoria, Rhodesia, 1966), pp. 1–4.

ately issued a statement disassociating themselves from this suggestion, which they saw as "a betrayal of the political cause of the Rhodesian African." [17] Chipunza replied that he was not suggesting a coalition but rather a national government in which all shades of opinion would be represented and which would be above party politics. But the damage had already been done. In June, Chipunza was banned from entering Zambia by the Zambian government because it saw him as an extension of the white Rhodesian system. In the ensuing publicity, Mhlanga withdrew his support from Chipunza and began to lobby against him as leader of the Opposition.[18] Toward the end of August, Chipunza miscalculated his party's patience. On the eve of the new parliamentary session he had still not called a party caucus, nor had he given any explanation for not doing so. On August 26, therefore, he was ousted by a majority vote of 7 (Mhlanga, Hlbangana, M'Kudu, Majongwe, Chigogo, Gondo, Behane) to 6.

Gondo returned as leader of the Opposition with Percy M'Kudu as deputy leader. Gondo maintained that since Chipunza had not called a party caucus, he had done so, and as a result, new officials were elected "pending the holding of a UPP Congress or Convention." Chipunza responded: "As far as I am concerned, I am still Leader and until they go about it in the proper way instead of running around trying to stab one in the back, I will continue. They have elected Gondo as Leader of their group." [19] However, on September 3, the Speaker of the House, A. R. W. Stumbles, officially recognized Gondo.

[17] This statement was published in the *Rhodesia Herald,* April 23, 1966.

[18] *Ibid.,* June 21, 1966.

[19] *Ibid.,* Sept. 1, 1966.

Under the Southern Rhodesian Ministerial and Parliamentary Salaries and Allowances Act, the leader of the Opposition is the parliamentarian who, in the opinion of the Speaker, is recognized by Parliament as the leader of the official opposition party. Chipunza accepted this ruling, but commented that his removal had been the work of a "clique."

At this point, M'Kudu begins to come into prominence within the party. In contrast to Chipunza's Zambian incident, M'Kudu's abortive attempt to join the Malawian delegation to the Organization of African Unity (OAU) enhanced his status because of the finesse with which he handled the whole situation.[20] The party operated under Gondo's leadership until January 1967, when the congress took place.

### *The Party Congress*

On December 16, 1966, Cephas Hlbangana of the UPP publicity committeee announced that the party would at last be holding its congress. By this time it had established approximately forty branches throughout the country and had three main offices, in Salisbury, Umtali, and Bulawayo. These three offices used up a "large percentage of the party levies." [21] The congress assembled on Saturday, January 21, with 130 delegates and 300 in attendance, at the Hellenic Hall in Gwelo. All had traveled at their own expense, since no party funds were available.[22] Ac-

[20] Hastings Banda, the president of Malawi, was said to be a major financial contributor to the UPP. "Always very sympathetic in a practical fashion, he advised the UPP to be constitutional," according to John Morgan.

[21] Percy M'Kudu, interview, Salisbury, Aug. 1, 1967.

[22] Annual party membership dues were 2/6 (35 cents).

cording to the party constitution, congress had to meet at least once a year, and those officially entitled to participate were: the president, two deputy presidents, the chairman, two deputy chairmen, the secretary, the treasurer, party members of the Rhodesian Parliament and prospective and adopted candidates, members of the standing committee, four members from each regional council, four delegates from the Women's Association, two delegates from the United People's Youth Wing, and three delegates from each branch.[23] Although the constitution mentioned a youth movement and a women's organization, there was no evidence that either of these had come into being. E. Mbobo, a former organizer of the RP and a member of the Mzilikazi branch of the UPP, summed up what the congress sought to do: "The choice of leaders was made 18 months ago by the Party's members of Parliament alone. They have quarreled and changed the leadership twice in the interim period and tomorrow a leader chosen by the Party members should be elected." [24]

For some time prior to this, Percy M'Kudu had showed further signs of the shrewdness and political acumen which was to enable him to win the position of leader of the Opposition in January 1967 and subsequently to retain it. At his own expense, he had begun traveling across the country to branch offices of the party, making himself and his ideas known to those who would be attending the congress. Then, on January 20, one day before the congress, he placed a half-page advertisement, "A New Year's Message to my Fellow Africans," in the *Rhodesia Herald*

[23] *United People's Party Constitution* (Salisbury: RCA, 1965), section 9, p. 5.

[24] *Rhodesia Herald,* Jan. 20, 1967.

at his own expense. This was a well-presented and well-reasoned statement on his own and the party's aspirations.

The congress rather than the parliamentary caucus now had an opportunity to decide who would lead the party. "We had to battle to keep the caucus from making decisions only the congress should," later commented John Morgan.[25] Of 121 votes for president cast by the party congress, M'Kudu received 58; Gondo, 26; Chipunza, 26; and Makaya, 11. The elected party executive was composed of M'Kudu (president), Gondo (vice-president), Mhlanga (party chairman), Makaya (secretary), Behane (treasurer), and Morgan (deputy party chairman).[26]

Thus a new party leadership had been selected by the party congress, there was a constitution, a party policy had begun to emerge, and there was a valid, though limited, base of operation.

### *The Registration of Voters Campaign, 1967: A Study of the Operational Difficulties of the UPP*

In the two and a half months following the party congress the UPP engaged in a major organizational and educational effort to both register and reregister African voters by April 8, 1967. There was a potential voter registration of 70,000 on the B roll and 9,000 on the A roll.[27] In September 1966, as a result of the Whitehead enrollment campaign, there were 10,827 Africans on the B roll and 2,360 on the A roll. By January 1967 there had been only 2,425 reregistrations and 346 new registrations. The *Rhodesia Herald* commented that despite Britain's

[25] Interview, Salisbury, Aug. 20, 1967.
[26] *Sunday Mail* (Salisbury), Jan. 22, 1967.
[27] *Rhodesia Herald*, Jan. 23, 1967.

desire for a return to constitutionality based on the 1961 constitution, African participation in politics was so limited that the only conclusion to be drawn was that Africans had withdrawn from constitutional politics.[28] But the UPP engaged in the campaign because, as John Morgan commented, "the best the UPP could have hoped for would have been a sufficient re-registration to win in five marginal urban constituencies where nonwhites would have tipped the balance."[29]

The UPP experienced several difficulties in this "Claim Your Vote" registration campaign. First, they operated on a limited budget (£500 was allocated for the postal vote section) and 10,000 forms were sent out by March 10. In addition, the petrol shortage meant restrictions on the amount of travel that could be done, although M'Kudu and the other members of the party tried to travel as widely as possible. Makaya said, "If we had jeeps, twenty-four to thirty [people] would be in Parliament in the opposition."[30] Furthermore, the forms themselves posed problems in terms of their complexity. Gondo commented: "During my recent visit to the African areas I was told, for example, they did not know why they have to fill in another form to re-register instead of just completing a card and giving their address."[31] Chiefs and headmen were automatically enrolled without registration after appointment by the Department of Internal Affairs; the relevant registering officers were informed and they were put on the roll.[32] Percy M'Kudu maintained that a

[28] *Ibid.* [29] Interview, Salisbury, Aug. 20, 1967.
[30] Interview, Salisbury, Aug. 14, 1967.
[31] Interview, Salisbury, Aug. 3, 1967.
[32] Chief registering officer (voters), interview, Aug. 11, 1967.

major obstacle to registering more voters was the impression "that by registering their vote, Africans would be demonstrating their support for the government"; in addition, African teachers had been influenced by ZANU-ZAPU broadcasts from Lusaka belittling the whole procedure.[33] Morgan pointed out that it was necessary for Africans to go to a commissioner of oaths or a justice of the peace for registration and that while whites could complete the process within five minutes, "the whole thing was made much more difficult for Africans—they were ignored or kept waiting for a long time—the black man was just not keen to go to a designated official to register." [34] Because of government restrictions, black politicians found it difficult to organize political campaigns in restricted rural areas where only minimal political activity was permitted and in urban areas where the scope of African political activities was limited.[35] As a result, only 5,228 Africans were on the B roll after the campaign.[36]

## *The UPP Engages in Governmental Criticism*

Although all of the African members of Parliament at this time shared similar social and educational backgrounds and patterns of political socialization and were roughly the same age, the UPP was far from being a mono-

[33] Percy M'Kudu, interview, Salisbury, Aug. 1, 1967.

[34] Interview, Salisbury, Aug. 20, 1967.

[35] *Rhodesia Herald,* June 13, 1969. There was little scope for canvassing because of government restrictions in 1966. In the 1969 referendum campaign, Isaac Samuriwo (independent) claimed that he had not been allowed to hold a meeting even in his own constituency under the policy of allowing no political meetings in Tribal Trust Lands. The white Centre Party also encountered such difficulties.

[36] *Hansard,* Aug. 30, 1968.

lithic structure. Thinking within the party ranged from the conservative to the quasi-nationalistic, and its members showed differing levels of political skill and represented different interests.

On some issues, such as "separate development," which aimed at introducing residential racial segregation to Rhodesia, there was unanimity among members of the Opposition. Behane said that the government had acted against the wishes of the great majority of Rhodesians of all races. Such a policy would lead to strife and the government would be well advised to change its intentions.

> We cannot dictate to people as to how and where they should live. . . . I do not see why there should be new legislation aimed at dividing Rhodesia because of colour, because colour itself is not the division. . . . Once legislation is aimed at working against the wills of the people or of stopping what people regard as a national right, people tend to fight against that legislation, and because of that, strife comes about, violence breaks out and eternal peace is broken.[37]

Chad Chipunza said that the people who most favored separate development were not people native to Rhodesia but those who had run away from their own countries and hoped to find a niche here. In Rhodesia separate development meant a policy of political domination by one race over another. Through it, the African would be completely cut off from the economic benefits of the country. On what was being spent out of the public funds the African was not getting a fair deal, and separate development was a policy to enable one section of the people to be exploited for the benefit of another.[38]

[37] *Ibid.*, July 26, 1967. [38] *Ibid.*

On another issue, however, what might be characterized as the right wing of the party—Rubatika, Chigogo, Kandengwa, and Behane—were strongly in favor of the government's restrictive legislation aimed at keeping law and order. Rubatika said, "We stand in admiration of the Government's stand in bringing about law and order. If by any eventuality the white man should fall, we must pay the price and I am prepared to tell them to shoot me because I am dedicated to a cause and I shall live and die by it." [39] Behane congratulated the minister of justice and law and order on the difference between conditions in the country in 1967 and those that prevailed in the late 1950's and early 1960's. In those days there was intimidation in the Tribal Trust areas and many Africans were faced with a reign of terror. ZAPU's periodical was particularly critical of African MP's and commented:

> The African Stooge Members of the rebel "parliament" were all praise for the Smith fascist forces as "dedicated men fighting to preserve peace among people in Matabeleland."
>
> We must warn that as long as these running dogs of white settler fascism persist in this direction they will remain in the eyes of Zimbabweans indistinguishable from Southern Africa fascists of the deepest dye who will be dealt with accordingly when the time comes. Their only salvation lies in their renouncing lucrative sell-out activities and taking their stand against fascist oppression.[40]

Both Chipunza and Hlbangana were strong and consistent critics of the government and can be classified as the party's left, that is, closest to the Nationalists; Gondo, Hove, Samuriwo, Makaya, Mhlanga, and Majongwe make

[39] *Ibid.* [40] *Zimbabwe News,* 2, no. 19 (Sept. 1967), 5.

up the center; M'Kudu, also in the center, functioned as a balance between the party's two wings. Government policy in such areas as African unemployment, the development of the Tribal Trust Lands, and immigration came under frequent attack by Chipunza and Hlbangana. They also often questioned cabinet ministers on controversial issues such as the welfare of Nationalists held in detention.

On the question of the condemnation of terrorism, there was also no party unanimity. In August 1967, Behane commented in the House that the security forces had done magnificent work against the communist infiltrators.[41] Patrick Rubatika said that all Rhodesians hated chaos and disorder and were prepared to stand together to prevent foreign infiltrators from trying to stir it up in Rhodesia, and P. E. Chigogo asked whether the infiltration was a trick by which Britain was hoping to establish that there was chaos in Rhodesia. Did the British want conditions like those in the Congo, and for that matter in Nigeria and Ghana? Chipunza and Hlbangana were silent. There was so much doubt as to the solidarity of the party on this issue that, on September 3, Percy M'Kudu issued a statement (presumably for party unity) that he and his party were solidly against terrorism in any country, and particularly in Rhodesia. "We are against terrorism when there is a European government in control, just as we would be against it when there is an African government in control." [42]

While some members of the UPP vigorously criticized the Rhodesian Front government on several important issues, the party's effectiveness was limited by the fact that it was not really in a bargaining position and, hence, not

[41] *Hansard,* Aug. 30, 1967. [42] *Rhodesia Herald,* Sept. 1, 1967.

able to force any compromises. Thus UPP criticism of the government cannot be characterized in terms of Lewis Coser's "conflict-integration dialectic," in which institutionalized conflict is a mechanism for adjustment of norms to new conditions, the translation of issues into objectives which can be achieved within the system.[43] In some instances the UPP might have been a restraining factor, but it was never any more than this. There is, therefore, considerable divergence from the traditional Western model in which the opposition party is a government-in-waiting. The UPP agreed on the rules of the game, sought offices in duly constituted elections, and formulated policies, but it represented interests in a way that was hardly conducive to checking power. Its primary role was, therefore, confined to providing a channel of information, and it lacked effectiveness and efficacy.

### *Rhodesian Front Attitudes toward the UPP*

Although the RF considered the UPP "rabble,"[44] it tolerated the UPP presence in Parliament for two reasons: (1) to sustain parliamentary procedure and a semblance of legality, and (2) in the sense of a "safety valve" with which the RF hoped to placate at least some African opposition. "That's how democracy works in Rhodesia. And men like Mr. Percy M'Kudu and his colleagues, who act constitutionally (however much they may oppose the government's views) are an important part of this democratic system which ensures justice and peace in our land."[45] But the

[43] Lewis Coser, *The Functions of Social Conflict* (Glencoe, Ill.: Free Press, 1964).

[44] John Morgan, interview, Salisbury, Aug. 20, 1967.

[45] *African Times*, Dec. 6, 1967.

RF continually tried to demonstrate that African and non-white politicians, even those working within the system, were not to be trusted. This view is epitomized by the case of the M.P. for the B-roll constituency of Magondi, Behaba Govan, an independent. In July 1967, Govan stated that the ministry of education had ordered the seizure of his new car, worth £780, for nonpayment of a £40 bill which had already been paid: "Mr. Govan, a member of the parliamentary select committee on education, said that the seizure of his car . . . was the culmination of a long series of mistakes in which the Ministry billed him £40 for another parent's school fees; sent his bills to the wrong address; credited a payment of £20 to another person's account; issued a summons against him. . . ."[46] Petty offenses such as abuses of petrol rationing by African M.P.'s also received widespread publicity, although such offenses were rampant in Rhodesia.

The *cause célèbre* was the resignation of Isaac Samuriwo from the UPP on August 3, 1967. Samuriwo was fined £500 on twenty-five counts of fraudulent submission of false parliamentary expense accounts totaling £300 for subsistence and traveling allowances between May 1965 and April 1967. Samuriwo had given his address as Parklands Farm, twenty-five miles from Salisbury, whereas he was actually living at Marimba Park, about nine miles from Salisbury. Chad Chipunza saw the position as follows: "When Mr. Samuriwo gave his farm as his home address, to him the farm was the most valuable asset he had, and having invested in it he felt that he had to look after it and so for practical purposes he considered this his home. No question of trying to earn a few pence—it was in good

[46] *Rhodesia Herald,* July 9, 1967.

faith."[47] An informant on the staff of the House of Assembly maintained that such abuses were commonplace even at the cabinet level but were never turned into major issues. Gondo said:

This is one of the RF efforts. . . . They would like the public, if not, in fact, the world outside, to think how irresponsible an African in Rhodesia is. . . . Even in my own case, when I discovered abuses in the sugar industry and went down to my constituency in the Triangle to investigate them, I found out that after I had left, people had been sent down to find out about my movements—with whom I talked, where I slept, what people told me, what they showed me. They were trying to build up a case.[48]

Clearly, then, while Samuriwo might, in the strictest sense, have acted fraudulently, if he had been white the issue would have been handled differently.

## *The UPP and the Nationalists*

The main difference between the UPP and the Nationalists was, in the words of UPP spokesman Gondo in 1967, that "at present the UPP is a party acting in politics and the ZANU and ZAPU are parties which are not acting at the moment." In a letter to the *London Daily Telegraph* on July 25, 1967, Percy M'Kudu wrote about his party's position regarding the Nationalists:

It has been alleged against my party that we represent very few Africans. This is not so, as all Africans are as one on major issues. The differences between the so-called Nationalists and the party I lead is that we use different ways of attaining our

[47] Interview, Salisbury, Aug. 29, 1967.
[48] Interview, Salisbury, Aug. 3, 1967.

goal. The Nationalists seek the shortest way via "one man–one vote." We take the practical way of transition measured by success—by merit and achievement, rather than by set time. But we all want majority rule and eventually one man–one vote.

Morgan said that while the UPP accepted the *Tiger* proposals, the Nationalists did not.[49] Some members of the party were violently opposed to the Nationalists; others clearly were not. Chad Chipunza, the best speaker and parliamentarian in the party, was the closest to the Nationalists. He grew up with Robert Mugabe of ZANU, was a colleague of Leopold Takawira of ZANU, a "friend" of Ndabaningi Sithole and Joshua Nkomo, with whom Herbert Chitepo of ZANU lived for six months after returning to Rhodesia from study abroad. The overt nationalist attitude to the UPP is summed up in W. D. Musarurwa's comment, "They will be like fourteen lean mice under the massive claws of a huge (50 strong) cat. Their only achievement will be the fat cheque that they bring home at the end of each month." [50]

Ndabaningi Sithole is said to have initiated an exchange of letters and ideas between himself and M'Kudu. The RF was aware of this exchange and accused the UPP of paying lip service to the Nationalists.[51] The minister of justice and law and order, Desmond Lardner-Burke, said that there seemed to be fear in the hearts of Opposition M.P.'s. They feared that if they talked in a way that the Nationalists did not approve, they would be in trouble.

49 Interview, Salisbury, Aug. 20, 1967.
50 *Central African Examiner,* June 1965, p. 9.
51 *Rhodesia Herald,* Aug. 18, 1967.

Consequently, they spoke so they were able to go to the Nationalists and say, "You see we support you." [52]

## *The UPP's* Raison d'Etre

How did members of the UPP view their roles in the politics of Rhodesia? Percy M'Kudu saw the Opposition in the following light: "We are participating because we were elected under the 1961 constitution, which has not been dissolved yet; we feel that our oath of allegiance is still the same as when elected and this entitles us to be in the House. The Opposition is serving a very useful function because we are the only way the African can be heard outside of Rhodesia because *Hansard,* at least, goes outside of the country." [53] Morgan maintained that they were keeping dialogue alive.[54] For Gondo, the UPP was a restraining force, even though a limited one, within the parliamentary system.

Morgan maintained that M'Kudu was, in practice, regularly consulted by members of the cabinet and of Parliament and was given governmental assistance in solving problems: "infinite help is given him by members who like him." [55] On practical matters such as health and education (the training of nurses, the establishment of schools, and so on), Makaya said that he handled a great number of problems for his constituents and entered a considerable amount of correspondence; his were mainly urban problems such as unemployment and housing shortages. Gondo mentioned that he was involved in the settling of two chieftainship succession disputes in his electoral district

[52] *Hansard,* Aug. 15, 1967.
[53] Interview, Salisbury, Aug. 1, 1967.
[54] Interview, Salisbury, Aug. 20, 1967. [55] *Ibid.*

and also handled personal and general problems for constituents and others. The UPP was also involved, as we have seen, in the attack against a new separate development bill and was regarded, in this instance, by members of both the Coloured and the Asian population as something of a rallying point—although it was only on this issue that their support was forthcoming. On all other issues, they gave no support to the UPP.

### *UPP Perceptions of Weaknesses in the Party*

Members of the party perceived the UPP's weaknesses to be primarily on an organizational level. Chipunza felt that "many of our people are just not politicians," and Morgan saw the level of debate as low. Solutions to the problem, as far as M'Kudu was concerned, involved "team work and good leadership capable of holding its own and accepting challenges." "We need a very high-powered organizer, one who understands about politics, one who would direct all activities. Once we have such a person, we could have branches in all the districts and he would direct public and other relations, both African and European, but it would be difficult to keep such a man without a higher retainer." [56] Gondo echoed this need and added that the party needed external advisers such as lawyers, but that many whites were afraid of getting into trouble. Morgan substantiated this fact and added that whites, especially big financial groups, were also afraid of suffering financial losses if they became too closely identified with the UPP. Morgan did mention that a group of white helpers kept headquarters alive, and he felt, furthermore, that there was a need for good organization and more white support. He

[56] Interview, Salisbury, Aug. 1, 1967.

also regretted that support was not coming from the Asians and Coloureds (except for isolated cases) because, he maintained, they would rather be under a white minority government than a black majority one. Chipunza saw a need for a leader "with inner drive and aptitude for settling personality disputes." Gondo saw a need to limit freedom of public expression by party members. "I agree a person is entitled to his own opinion. You cannot say so and so must act in a way, but in matters of principle and policy statement, party policy, party politics—then there should be no difference." He also said that the apathy of the black middle class (businessmen and property owners) was a major problem: "We have to get our people ready and prepared to achieve by any available means . . . what is available to us today. One man–one vote can only be given to the people by an African government. I do not believe for a moment that the white government in this country, the RF or any other government, can give it." [57]

Most realistically of all, Chad Chipunza summed up the position: "The African people as a people must realize the needs and then real leadership will emerge—which must transcend cliques and parties. I hope there is still an opportunity for Africans to put their heads together." [58]

### *Fragmentation*

In August 1968, Chad Chipunza, by now tired of playing a secondary role in the party, resigned from the UPP and joined the newly formed Democratic Party (DP) as its only

[57] Interviews with Morgan, Chipunza, and Gondo, Salisbury, Aug. 1967.

[58] Interview, Salisbury, Aug. 29, 1967.

parliamentary representative. The chairman of the DP was Walter Mukahlera, a former member of ZAPU,[59] which meant that Chipunza was ideologically more at home. Among other things, the DP sought the abolition of the Land Apportionment Act and aimed at "one man–one vote."

In October two members of the right wing of the UPP left the party, apparently dissatisfied with M'Kudu's leadership. In justification of their action they cited Prime Minister Harold Wilson's comment that the poor state of African leadership in Rhodesia was not helping Britain to reach a constitutional settlement, although, clearly, the dichotomy between their thinking and that of other members of the party was the underlying cause of their withdrawal.

The referendum of June 1969, to determine whether Rhodesia was to become a republic and to decide on the new constitutional proposals, viscerally affected the UPP. The new constitution would not allow for multiracial parties, since it emphasized parliamentary representation by race. The lower house would consist of sixteen seats, eight for the Tribal Trust Lands and eight for African voters in urban areas with slightly higher qualifications than the B roll. M'Kudu led his party's campaign against the implementation of this constitution; in the *Rhodesia Herald* of June 7, 1969, he said that many chiefs had expressed to him their dissatisfaction with the new constitution, claiming that they did not want parliamentary duties. In addition, he reassured white voters that even if there were a successful "no" vote on the republican referendum and Africans eventually did achieve political power, "what

59 *Manchester Guardian,* Sept. 5, 1968.

had happened in the Congo, Zambia and Tanzania would not take place in Rhodesia."

On June 18, 1968, at a meeting in Salisbury attended by more than 400 people, M'Kudu, after discussing the implications of the forthcoming referendum, hinted at a possible *rapprochement* with the DP. He must have realized that there was little hope of swaying the white electorate and that an effort should be made to avoid further fragmentation of the African Opposition, particularly with an important general election less than a year away. Immediately after the referendum, on June 20, the merger of the UPP and the DP into a new party, the National People's Union (NPU), was announced at a meeting in Rusape.

The equipment and facilities of the UPP were to be used by the NPU. Gordon Chavanduka was the president of the new party [60] and Percy M'Kudu was vice-president and leader of the Opposition in Parliament. Mhlanga did not join the party, but commented, "I will serve my people as an independent." [61]

Toward the end of August, it became clear that there was already discontent in the NPU. Chipunza had set his sights on the leadership of the party in Parliament for several reasons: first, he had once held the position in the UPP and enjoyed the prestige the job carried; second, the special allowance for the leader of the Opposition was financially enticing to him; and, third, he hoped to be a

[60] Chavanduka, then thirty-seven years old, has a B.A. from the University of California and an M.A. from Manchester (England) in sociology. He is currently a lecturer in sociology at the University College of Rhodesia.

[61] *Rhodesia Herald,* June 20, 1969.

more aggressive parliamentary leader than M'Kudu who essentially balanced factions within the party. A meeting on August 27, under the chairmanship of Gordon Chavanduka, resulted in a realignment. Chipunza was chosen as the new leader of the NPU.[62]

M'Kudu, from the start, was unhappy with Chipunza's leadership, and on August 30 he resigned from the parliamentary caucus—but not from the party or from his post as vice-president.[63] By September 15, however, he decided to resign from the NPU and to sit in the House as an independent.

The pragmatism of the UPP was the main legacy carried over into the NPU; while the long-term aims of the NPU included majority rule, the party nonetheless decided to operate within the racially restrictive framework of the new constitution. Chavanduka opposed the constitutional proposals because they "favored the perpetuation and increase of racialism and tribalism," [64] but in the absence of alternatives he chose to operate within the redefined white system. The Opposition, then, differed over dominant goals but operated within and sustained the given system.[65] It consented to the parameters of the system and the rules of the game within that system.

In the April 1970 election the NPU was defeated as a

[62] The parliamentary caucus was composed of Chipunza, Gondo, M'Kudu, Majongwe, Samuriwo, Rubatika, Kandengwa, Hove, and Hlbangana. Behane and Chigogo, who had withdrawn from the UPP, refused to attend the caucus, and Mhlanga and Makaya saw themselves as independents.

[63] *Rhodesia Herald,* Aug. 30, 1969.

[64] *Ibid.,* June 27, 1969.

[65] See Otto Kirchheimer, "Germany, the Vanishing Opposition," in *Political Opposition in Western Democracies,* Robert Dahl, ed. (New Haven: Yale University Press, 1966), p. 237.

party, the multiracial Centre Party successfully winning seven of the eight African seats (although it won none of the white seats it contested). The Centre Party, under the leadership of Patrick Bashford, ironically, emerged as an offshoot of the Rhodesian Constitutional Association.

By their own definition, the UPP and NPU must be seen, then, as opposition parties working within the framework of the Rhodesian political system and to some extent fulfilling the roles traditionally associated with an opposition party. However, they cannot be defined as potential governments. Their level of operation was based on institutionalized opposition, "examining and criticizing what the government has done and proposes to do . . . questioning ministers in the House, through motions of censure and no confidence, through the debates that accompany the passing of financial legislation and so on." [66]

They were tolerated by the white power structure for three reasons: (1) because of their lack of effectiveness and efficacy, (2) because they functioned as a safety valve, and (3) for the sake of constitutionality. The parties lacked the anchor points of ideology and strict policy goals that were the hallmarks of both the Nationalists and the RF. Their *modus operandi* was determined by the politics of survival rather than by ideological dogmatism. Their significance was the fact that some Africans were prepared to work inside the Rhodesian constitutional system.

[66] K. C. Wheare, *Modern Constitutions,* 2d ed. (London: Oxford University Press, 1966), p. 118.

CHAPTER 10

# The Centre Party

The Centre Party came into existence in 1969 when a group of white Rhodesians, many of whom had gone into opposition with Sir Edgar Whitehead, decided to regroup. The inaugural congress of the Centre Party, attended by 250 delegates, was held in the Andy Miller Hall, Bulawayo, in April 1969. The congress was opened by the former Speaker of the Federal Parliament, Sir Ian Wilson. The emergence of the CP as a multiracial political party is ironic in that after the 1962 election many of its members had felt it was impossible for the Rhodesia Party to operate with African parliamentary representation. While the Centre Party itself was to suffer the same fate as the Rhodesia Party, with no white members returned to Parliament, the subsequent structure of the party was in this instance to remain multiracial. Patrick Bashford, one of the founding members and leader of the CP, told the delegates to the congress that the party stood for racial cooperation and racial growth.[1] Yet at the same congress, the party accepted the continuation of the Land Apportionment Act and made clear that it did not intend to integrate government schools. It did, however, emphasize

[1] Officers of the Centre Party included Sir Richard Sullivan as chairman, Arthur Sarif and Nick McNally as vice-presidents, E. Greenfield as political secretary, and N. E. Watungwa as the deputy leader.

that there was to be no discrimination in business and industrial areas and that it would seek to eliminate obvious examples of racial discrimination.[2]

In a later publication, *Settle for Sanity,* the Centre Party elaborated on its basic principles. Rhodesia was to have a representative democracy (based on a qualified franchise) to meet the common needs and aspirations of all Rhodesians. Racial discrimination was to be decreased progressively whenever and wherever it could be done without causing or increasing racial tension; advancement was to be on merit. Specifically, the CP's franchise proposal retained the A-roll qualifications and left substantially unchanged the proportion of B-roll seats; it did, however, introduce a form of permanent representation for both major races in Parliament, and a Declaration of Rights with safeguards against the repeal of entrenched clauses protecting African rights.

By November 1969 the Centre Party had begun to consolidate some of its policy goals and also its attitude toward settlement with Britain. A publication issued by the party office, *A Blueprint for Rhodesia,* stated that the CP pledged itself to build the "new" Rhodesia on economic expansion, full employment, and education. It would maintain the standards of life, the quality of administration, and the law and order which Rhodesia needed. It would work within the constitution of Rhodesia, secure free trade with the nations of the world, and work in close cooperation with neighboring states in southern Africa. Within Rhodesia it planned to work with the leaders of the African people "without bowing to black nationalism."

While advocating greater African participation in the

2 *Rhodesia Herald,* April 15, 1969.

political system, in actuality the Centre Party was not far removed from the Rhodesian Front. It intended to work within the constitution of Rhodesia, to work with African leaders but not African nationalist leaders, to maintain the prevailing standards of life and the existing concepts of law and order. According to A. J. P. Graham, a member of the Highlands North constituency, the Centre Party believed "in the continuation of civilized rule in Rhodesia for a lot longer than Mr. Smith's lifetime. Its politics would secure international recognition of Rhodesia's independence, restoration of international trade, a progressive improvement of the lot of all sections of the population and 'a permanent and prosperous place in this country for all of us.' "[3]

In preparing to contest the 1970 general election, the party encountered several organizational difficulties; it was refused permission to go into the Tribal Trust Lands, and, in certain instances, public meetings were prohibited in African townships.[4] It also had to contend with whisper campaigns, for example, that the party was "run by Jews."[5]

Financially, the Centre Party was in a considerably better position than any of the African parties. In terms of office space, staff, equipment, and general political know-how, it was an organized political party. It had a large budget for political advertisements, branch offices in all the major cities in Rhodesia, and a well-organized women's section. The Rhodesian press, especially the *Rhodesia Herald,* favored the CP both editorially and in terms of news coverage.

[3] *Ibid.,* May 14, 1969. [4] *Ibid.,* May 10, 1969.

[5] *Ibid.,* May 30, 1969. It should be emphasized, however, that liberal Catholics probably played the most decisive role in the organization.

Supporters of the party included many members of the Rhodesian establishment, such as Evan Campbell, former high commissioner in London; John Foggin, a former under-secretary in the ministry of internal affairs; Sir Richard Sullivan; and Maureen Watson, a former M.P. The political skills and energy of many capable women, such as Muriel Rosen, a former Federal M.P., and Sheila Noland, were of extreme importance in the election campaign and subsequently as political advisors to the African M.P.'s.

Within limited scope, the Centre Party was attempting to rally constitutional opposition based on interracial solidarity, and Africans were urged to support the party. "If the African people choose to go it alone by joining an all-African political party—which is what the Rhodesian Front wants them to do—then there is very little hope for them. They would command only 16 seats in the Assembly for the foreseeable future and at least 23 seats are needed to block further retrogressive amendments to the Constitution. Seven European and 16 African seats would be a viable opposition." [6] Party leader Patrick Bashford expressed his view: "I do not see how the National People's Union (the official opposition at present) which has no European support, or any other all-African political party, can have any hope of success." [7]

### *Parliamentary Candidates*

Like the African members of the United People's Party, the African members of the CP were mainly from the middle class, and were either teachers or small businessmen. Ronald Sadomba, representative of the Nemakonde con-

[6] *Rhodesia Herald,* Sept. 16, 1969. [7] *Ibid.,* Sept. 17, 1969.

stituency, was the youngest member at the age of thirty-three (in 1972), and W. S. Moraka of the Matojeni constituency was the oldest at fifty-three. All had received missionary educations. Lewis A. Ndholvu of the Insukamini constituency had been employed in government service as a senior interpreter and recorder for the Rhodesian railways. Sadomba was a schoolteacher; Edward Watungwa, Harare representative, had been a schoolteacher and had also done public-relations work for the city of Salisbury; Micha Bhebe and Moraka were also schoolteachers (Bhebe represented Notshonaianga). Finally, Joel Mahalangu, a teacher, represented Mpopoma, and Lazarus Masenda the Mabuazuwa area.

Unlike the Nationalists, all these men lacked university-level education and in most instances were not financially independent. The assistance of well-educated white party officials with considerable parliamentary experience must, however, be seen as a balancing factor in any comparison with the UPP.

The white candidates presented by the party for A-roll seats in the 1970 general election represented the broad spectrum of the white Rhodesian middle class.[8] The RF

[8] Sam Gelman, a dairy farmer and businessman, opposed Prime Minister Smith for the Umzingwone constituency; G. Taylor, a farmer, ran for the Umtali West constituency; Patrick Bashford, for Borrowdale; Arthur Sarif, Bulawayo East; Shelia Noland, Highlands North; S. Howard, Raylton; J. Stakesby Lewis, Bulawayo district; G. H. Tanser, the chief education officer in Salisbury, Salisbury North; H. Norton, a land surveyor for the Rhodesian Railways, Hillside (Bulawayo constituency); Nick McNally, an advocate, opposed the minister of defense and external affairs (Howman) for the Mount Pleasant seat; J. Lamb opposed Jack Mussett, minister of commerce and industry, for the Umtali East constituency; A. P. Knottenbelt, the former headmaster at Fletcher High School for

candidates received 39,066 votes; CP candidates, 5,619; independents, 4,514; RA, 1,633; from a total of 86,420 registered voters on the European roll. A total of 8,326 voters were registered on the African roll; CP candidates received 2,147 votes; NPU, 1,000; independents, 747; RAP, 301; UPP, 133.

In all constituencies the number of registered African voters was small. Furthermore, less than 50 per cent of the registered voters actually voted on election day. The tables for the urban constituency of Harare and for the smaller constituency of Mpopoma indicate this position.

Harare

| CP | NPU | AAPP | Independent |
|---|---|---|---|
| (E. E. Watungwa) | (G. Muchado) | (M. D. Matimba) | (Patrick Rubatika) |
| 527 | 153 | 63 | 119 |

| | |
|---|---|
| Majority | 374 |
| Spoilt papers | 45 |
| Percentage of poll | 60.27 |

(Total number of registered voters: 1,505)

---

Africans at Gwelo, contested thc Arundel seat, opposing Brigadier Andrew Skeen; Group Captain Edmund Nelson, a former federal M.P., opposed Dr. Colin Barlow for Avondale; and finally, Jeremy Broome, an attorney, contested the Highland South constituency. Knottenbelt was born in 1913 in South Africa; Nelson was born in England and had farmed in Rhodesia for twenty-two years before becoming involved in the elections; Norton was born in South Africa; Mrs. Noland was born in Washington, D.C., and arrived in Rhodesia in 1956; Broome was born in 1919 in England and was educated at Winchester College; Sarif was born in Bulawayo in 1915; Howard was born in London and had resided in Rhodesia since 1951; Lewis was born in Johannesburg and was a retired civil servant who had lived in Rhodesia since 1937; Bashford was born in London in 1915 and had resided in Rhodesia since 1938; and McNally was born in Rhodesia in 1931 and attended school in South Africa.

| CP (L. J. Mahlangu) | RAP (R. T. Chigumira) | Mpopoma Independent (C. C. Chiremba) | Independent (A. C. Mutasa) | Independent (C. Hlbangana) |
|---|---|---|---|---|
| 174 | 38 | 60 | 54 | 67 |

| | |
|---|---|
| Majority | 107 |
| Spoilt papers | 4 |
| Percentage of poll | 75.51 |

(Total number of registered voters: 539)

## *The Centre Party in Parliament*

At the first meeting of Parliament following the 1970 election the prestige of the party was dealt a severe blow when the Rhodesian government refused to recognize the leader of the Centre Party, or anyone else, as the leader of the Opposition.[9] Desmond Lardner-Burke summed up the government's position: In the last Parliament, various groupings among the fifteen African M.P.'s were recognized as the official opposition. These M.P.'s had been elected on a common roll by all sections of the community. This was not the case now, he said. All the African M.P.'s in the Republican Parliament had been elected to represent Africans either on the African rolls or those in the Tribal Trust areas. "So how can they be called the opposition?" the minister asked. "I think it would be entirely wrong to seat an opposition based entirely on race." He added that an opposition which the Rhodesian Front would recognize need not in fact belong to a multiracial party. He believed the country would remain without an official opposition until the next general election. An opposition

[9] A group of eight tribally elected members formed themselves into the Rhodesian Electoral Union (REU) after their election. They were not a party in the normally accepted sense. Makaya was designated leader of the group.

should constitute a government-in-waiting formed by a party where support by the electorate was reflected in membership of the House.[10]

The African members of the Centre Party were, on the whole, more articulate in their parliamentary presentations and more pertinent in the questions they posed than any of the African parties had been. Part of the explanation for this is, of course, the fact that outside of Parliament there was a competent political staff and adequate financial resources. Patrick Bashford, Nick McNally, Shelia Noland, and many others helped research parliamentary problems, draft speeches, and organize committee meetings.[11] In addition, they assisted in the general administration of the Centre Party itself and in the publication of a monthly newspaper, *Centre Point*.

The range of topics examined was at all times well within the constitutional framework of parliamentary opposition. While the Centre Party, like its predecessors, cannot be seen as a government-in-waiting in the British parliamentary sense, it nevertheless served a valuable purpose by challenging and questioning the Rhodesian Front government. It kept governmental channels open for Africans and frequently defused tense political situations or made the RF more cautious in its policies.[12]

[10] *Rhodesia Herald,* July 25, 1970.

[11] There was at one point criticism of the Centre Party for being led by Europeans. In the February 1971 issue of *Centre Point,* Micha Bhebe responded to the criticism by saying, "We in the C.P. have a non-racial policy, for we believe that as Rhodesia is a multi-racial country, its future salvation lies in a multi-racial approach. The question of who is leader is thus decided on merit and in the spirit of a non-racial approach."

[12] A draft of the Residential Property Owners (Protection) Bill was released at a press conference in Salisbury on November 26,

Admittedly, it may be maintained that the Centre Party was little more than a "dummy opposition." Nevertheless, members of the party introduced important topics into the parliamentary debates and posed significant questions to various ministers. Ronald Sadomba, for example, questioned the minister of justice concerning the suspicious circumstances surrounding the death of Leopold Takawira of ZANU and was frequently concerned with the well-being of African nationalist leaders detained without trial. He also asked the government to introduce legislative measures to assist relatives of those detained for political reasons. While Sadomba's principal concerns were with the detainees, law and order, and civil rights, he was also interested in African education and unemployment.

Masenda emphasized incidents of racial prejudice, particularly problems encountered by African members of Parliament and their wives at restaurants outside of the major cities. His general interests focused on specific needs in the Tribal Trust Lands, such as roads, African education, and African health services. There was considerable emphasis by Edward Watungwa on international matters; he was quite critical of the government's role in perpetuating a state of illegality. "I hope the honourable members of this House know that the reason for our having no place in the world community is because of the actions of the government. Personally, I think we have taken a rebellious action and therefore have to consider whether we have to

1970, by the minister of local government and housing, Mark Partridge. The bill provided that residential areas in Rhodesia which were traditionally European, Asian, or Coloured could be declared exclusively for the use of any one of these communities. A statement issued by the opposition Centre Party vigorously attacked the bill and sustained strong opposition to it.

come back to legality." Watungwa was particularly concerned with the voiceless predicament of Africans in negotiations with Great Britain. "There is a feeling amongst our people that there is nothing government can do. I would like to go further. . . . There is a feeling amongst our people that government is only interested in serving one section of the people. There is a feeling amongst our people that there is nothing government can do because of the constitutional arrangement of this country, which has given 5,000,000 people 16 representatives and only 228,000 white people 50 representatives in this House." [13]

Other issues of particular interest to Watungwa included questions of African health, problems encountered by African students and rural Africans, and costs of traveling to and from African schools. Watungwa was extremely active in Parliament and tried to widen the participation of Africans in the civil service and to obtain some form of direct African representation in the urban areas.

Micha Bhebe introduced a wide range of specific problems, including the establishment of multiracial schools, increases in African teachers' salaries, relations with Malawi, Rhodesian military involvement with South Africa, the Land Tenure Act, the number of Africans permitted to hold public-service jobs, and the whole matter of sanctions.

Perhaps the most sophisticated of all the African M.P.'s, Josiah Gondo, who had several years of parliamentary experience, was not a member of the Centre Party. Specifically, Gondo was concerned with the registration of African voters, urban advisory boards, African secondary schools, African teachers' salaries, African police appoint-

[13] *Hansard,* June 3, 1970.

ments, the extention of the State Emergency Act, and the international predicament in Rhodesia.

*The Rhodesian Front and the Centre Party*

In a meeting with Smith, CP caucus leader Bhebe raised a number of significant issues. He was disturbed that the majority of the African people fell under the direct administration of the ministry of internal affairs, whose secretary had publicly identified himself with the philosophy of apartheid. Bhebe asked what reassurance the government was prepared to give the African people that it had abandoned its policy of provincialization, which they were convinced was disguised apartheid; what steps were being taken to restore the confidence of the tribal people in the district commissioners; and what plans had been made to develop the Tribal Trust Lands. In relation to the settlement proposals he asked how the annual $10 million earmarked for African development was to be spent; whether the government would give a categorical assurance that it would never seek to have the Declaration of Rights rendered nonjusticiable again; if the proposals were accepted by the people as a whole, would the government grant an amnesty to present restrictees and detainees; would the government amend the Electoral Act in respect of former detainees' voting rights and right to stand as candidates; and what were the government's intentions concerning those under the sentence of death.

An important byelection in August of 1971 involved the Mabelreign seat. The party's vice-president, Nick McNally, declared that if the CP did not at least manage to come in second in the election he would resign. Although the CP came at the bottom of the poll, he subsequently decided to carry on. But had he quit, few would have blamed him. The prospects for a multiracial party in a country whose politics had become increasingly polarized racially were dim. Many white Rhodesians—including Ian Smith—thought that the party was dangerously left-wing. But "we can't let our African members down at this stage by going out of business," Patrick Bashford declared.[14]

### *The Centre Party and Settlement*

In its January 1972 issue, *Centre Point* drew up what it referred to as a "balance sheet" on the settlement proposals. It emphasized first of all that the settlement was a compromise which should be regarded as a whole, or as a "package deal," and that a decision should be made on the settlement rather than on the acceptability of specific points; the choice was between "this settlement and no settlement at all." "If we want to reject this settlement we must say, 'we do not want this settlement, we want no settlement. We want to carry on with the 1969 Constitution as it is and with sanctions as they are.' So the question is, is this compromise settlement better than no settlement at all."

Among the arguments in favor of settlement in their balance sheet were: there would be quicker political advancement for Africans under the settlement terms than under the 1969 constitution; there would be more rapid economic advancement for Africans, more educated opposition, and more jobs with the removal of sanctions. All racially discriminatory laws and practices of discrimination by public officials were outlawed by the settlement pro-

[14] Quoted in "Multiracialists in Rhodesia Lose Heart," *Star,* (Johannesburg) Aug. 21, 1971.

posals; fundamental human rights were protected by the courts under a strong Declaration of Rights; appointments and promotion in civil service were to be based on merit rather than on race; amendments to the constitution would require a two-thirds majority of members of both houses of Parliament, including a majority of the Africans and Europeans of the House of Assembly counted separately.

Among the arguments against the political settlement were that the Centre Party was aware that under optimal conditions majority rule would take sixty-four years, and that substantial economic benefits might not reach Africans. Also, the continuation of sanctions might force white Rhodesians to negotiate on more favorable terms with Africans in the future. The Centre Party seemed unaware of the limitations of the Declaration of Rights and that appointments and promotions needed more than a mere paper statement. It was perhaps overly optimistic in its belief that the settlement proposals created "a new opportunity for the African people to register as voters, to elect their representatives to Parliament, and to take part in the political life of the country." [15]

After debating the pros and cons, the Centre Party expressed its support for the settlement terms, but with deep reservations. Patrick Bashford said, "We accept the Anglo-Rhodesian settlement proposals under duress." [16] Bhebe was doubtful on certain points of the settlement from the outset, but he did not want to see it rejected as a whole. "It would be futile to push these things through when they have been rejected by so many Africans. If Britain makes a settlement of this kind and does not keep control of this country, it will mean it has thrown off the Africans for-

[15] *Centre Point,* Jan. 1972.

[16] *Times* (London), Jan. 27, 1972.

ever."[17] In a conversation with Bhebe, Lord Pearce explained, "our task is to find out whether this package—with the parts you like and the parts you don't like—is acceptable as a whole." Bhebe replied, "I can say categorically that we are in favor of the proposals." "But that is no good," Lord Pearce returned. "We cannot give you assurances. This is a judgment you as Rhodesians have to make."[18]

In the final analysis, Bashford perceived of the settlement as the only "sober solution," although he continued to have grave doubts.

We know only too well the political dangers inseparable from conferring legality upon those who have shown such little regard for the rule of law. We fully realize the dubious value of solemn assurances uttered by men to whom oaths of allegiance are but scraps of paper to be torn up at will. . . . We are only too aware of the tenuous value of an agreement that represents a complete reversal of Rhodesian Front principles and politics, which has neither been debated in Parliament, nor indeed ratified by a Congress of the Rhodesian Front Party.

But on balance Bashford said the Centre Party accepted that Britain had done all it could, short of force, to bring about constitutional reform, and he could do no more than record the Party's acceptance of "Hobson's choice."[19]

Party member Taylor expressed a more conservative view. "God help the whites of this country if the embittered Africans, suffering under the control of a monolithic white block, were to be let loose on them. The desire to get their own back would be so great the consequences would be appalling." The settlement, he said, would offer

[17] *Ibid.* [18] *Ibid.* [19] *Star* (Johannesburg), Jan. 29, 1972.

"some very slight hope" that the people of Rhodesia could divide on political lines rather than racial ones.[20]

*The Centre Party and the African National Council*

The CP's position in the political spectrum and its major limitations were apparent in Bashford's statement that the Centre Party believed in a "meaningful policy of advancement on merit." [21] It is of particular interest that with the emergence of the African National Council, the Centre Party had to contend with a strong and viable African opposition to its left—an opposition that was not only competing for potential African membership but was also beginning to draw away CP parliamentarians such as Sadomba, who resigned from the Centre Party not because he questioned the loyalty and honesty of the members of the party but rather because he opposed its stand on the settlement proposals.[22]

In the March 1972 issue of *Centre Point,* the party posed various questions to the ANC: You complain that the proposals postpone African majority rule; when can you offer the Africans majority rule? You complain that the proposals do not abolish racial discrimination; what are you doing to remove racial discrimination? You complain that the aid offered will not help Africans; how many jobs, how many houses, how much land can you offer to the African of Rhodesia, and when? Does the ANC want peace and prosperity, or does it just want personal power?

On the extreme right of the spectrum, Bashford saw the new United Front. In his estimation, it was only able

[20] *Times* (London), Jan. 27, 1972. [21] *Centre Point,* April 1972.
[22] *Ibid.,* Feb. 1972.

to "rant and rave about separate development." [23] On the extreme left, there was the ANC cry of "one man–one vote," which to him appeared equally unacceptable as a viable political alternative. He saw the Rhodesian Front in equivocal terms, "in its vain attempt to be all things to all whites at the expense of everyone else."

Bashford perceived of the Centre Party as a "democratic institution." [24] He reasoned that the policies of the party reflected the ideas of its members in that its leaders were elected at an annual party congress. He juxtaposed his party with the Rhodesian Front Party, which he considered the official organization in a one-party authoritarian state. He felt that the ANC approaches had been tried in other parts of Africa and had failed. The Centre Party, however, offered policies of "sane gradualism" which were reflected in the settlement proposals.

The real dilemma of the Centre Party was the fact that its constituency was predominantly white. "Moderate" Africans who were either attracted to the party as members or as parliamentary representatives may have identified with it only in the absence of alternatives. While the Centre Party offered a less extreme form of racialism in its political platform than the RF, it nonetheless did not consider all Africans eligible for the vote, hence its criticism of the ANC's policy of "one man–one vote." Rhodesian politics have always been the politics of the extreme. In a country where a white minority is able to wield wide controls over a black majority, there is little scope for half measures.

Because of this, Bashford was incorrect in his assumption that to date Rhodesians have allowed themselves to be

[23] *Ibid.*, April 1972. [24] *Ibid.*

talked out of properly trying policies of gradual advancement; he considered that in Sir Edgar Whitehead's day, African nationalism had led the country down, while today white chauvinism was to blame. Bashford seemed unaware of the central reality of Rhodesian politics, that there was no place for "sane gradualism" or "moderation" in a highly polarized political context.

The Centre Party backed the settlement proposals because they involved concessions by the Smith government and would open the way to continued constitutional negotiation. "The Centre Party's recommendation was that because Rhodesia was on 'a slippery slope' further prolongation of the Anglo-Rhodesian dispute would only accelerate the slide into apartheid."[25] Indeed, a Centre Party delegation led by Bashford met Sir Alec Douglas-Home in London on May 1, 1972, and asked Britain to implement the settlement proposals regardless of the Pearce Commission's findings, since to abandon the proposals would aggravate racial relations and worsen the situation of Rhodesian Africans. Furthermore, the party considered that the African viewpoint was not being ignored; "on the contrary we could see more clearly than he could what would be beneficial to him and his success."[26] This was a surprisingly naïve statement since there were few guarantees that the Smith government, having once settled the constitutional issue, would not immediately entrench itself and implement a separatist line. The statement had clear paternalistic undertones in its condescending view of African political responsibility.

In its estimation of the emerging support and strength of the ANC, the Centre Party's view was remarkably sim-

[25] *Ibid.*, May 1972. [26] *Ibid.*

ilar to that of the Rhodesian Front. It ignored the deep-rooted African discontent which surfaced after many years of silence because of the opportunities provided by the Pearce Commission. "The militants of the ANC, unwilling to see the wood for the trees, and seeking present advantage at the cost of future misery, were able to take advantage of the formalities implicit in a judicial examination by staging a rejection of the proposals." [27]

In a surprising moment of introspective self-examination, the party did admit that "it is perhaps not to our credit, as liberals, in touch with African opinion, that we were taken by surprise by this reversal of what had seemed to be the happy trend towards the introduction of much of what we had been working towards." [28]

Having made this somewhat remarkable admission, the party statement once again became ambivalent: "how delighted we would be to become a real buffer between the RF and the ANC. If Europeans then who could no longer stick the dictatorship of the Front would shake off their lethargy and join the Centre Party, while Africans who could see that the ANC was hell-bent for trouble would come along and join a moderate party, a strong multiracial opposition might take its place in Parliament." [29]

The Centre Party's inability either to relate to the white power elite or to align itself with manifestations of African nationalism is the root of its political ineffectiveness. Although it must be seen as more than a mere pressure group because of its efforts at political socialization, recruitment, and organization, it was never a viable government-in-waiting. Bashford was well aware of this limitation, and he felt that "in short, we need no less than a

[27] *Ibid.* [28] *Ibid.* [29] *Ibid.*

government-in-waiting." [30] Because of its ideological position, however, there seems little likelihood that this will ever happen.

[30] *Ibid.*, April 1972.

CHAPTER 11

# Rhodesia or Zimbabwe: Conflict or Coexistence?

The history of racial interaction in Rhodesia for the relatively short period from the first white settlement in 1890 until the present has been one of point-counterpoint; as Africans aspired to greater political participation, the white system deliberately and consciously escalated the requirements for meaningful involvement and placed it beyond their grasp. Most white Rhodesians viewed African political ambition as a severe threat to their privileged position. There was, therefore, a continual entrenchment of white political control and of concomitant African frustration: African equality simply implied white exclusion.

The white establishment might have broadened and maintained some of its power by absorbing members of the African elite into its ranks and allocating them rewards and status. In this way the African elite might have been diverted from potential involvement in conflict politics and incorporated into the constitutional process. Over the years there were African leaders of stature who would have been willing to participate if meaningful opportunities had been made available. However, in the tense multiracial situation, this was never feasible. The white establishment has seemed unable to differentiate between extreme militancy and legitimate political involvement. The solidification of the white world view underscores this fundamental irreconcilability; resolution of the inherent conflict would call for a visceral reordering of philosophical perspective, and most white Rhodesians seem either unable or unwilling to change.

Ian Smith epitomizes white Rhodesian intransigence, which is widespread; despite the conclusions of the Pearce Commission, he considers that the elimination of "racial discrimination" would be disastrous for both blacks and whites; the abandonment of high standards for whites and "a drop to the present level of Africans would mean the rapid disappearance of white leadership from the Rhodesian scene." He argues that merit, and not color, should be the criterion of a man's advancement: "We do not deny that certain of this legislation also benefits the European, and does afford him some protection for his standards of living and his way of life—which differs from that of the African. After the contribution he has made to the commonweal, I wonder if this is not fully justified." [1]

The constitutional solutions that have been formulated, time and time again (such as A and B voters' rolls, with differing weight attached to African and white votes), have merely sought to appease Britain or to pacify Africans and have always fallen far short of full African political participation. All of the formulas have been inherently flawed by the contradiction inherent in consulting Africans in order to bring about African exclusion.

The limitations placed on parliamentary opposition groups such as the United People's Party and the Centre Party and the restraints placed on the African National Council clearly indicate that the white Rhodesian political

[1] *Star* (Johannesburg), Aug. 4, 1973.

system is unwilling to regard them as anything more than necessary tokens. While these parties have selected personnel for leadership, formulated public policy, criticized the government, attempted limited political education of their supporters, and, on occasion, successfully intervened between the government and individuals, they have never been a challenge to the governing apparatus and have been tolerated by the RF because of Britain's concern for constitutionality and because none of the parties have posed real threats to the continued existence of the white presence. Furthermore, within the limits of qualified participation, these parties have been useful in introducing inputs into an otherwise closed system. The important question remains whether, by so doing, they have contributed to the maintenance of the equilibrium of the system and obviated the need for a more extensive form of African representation.

A constitutional settlement aimed at reconciling African and white interests is by its very nature a contradiction, even with some African acceptance of the terms. Such a settlement would merely legitimize the Unilateral Declaration of Independence, continue white control, and place in white hands the manipulation of the pace of African advancement. As a result of the Pearce Commission's findings of widespread African discontent, however, it seems unlikely that a fictitious African acceptance, whether generated by the RF or not, could now sway Britain into granting full independence.

Future trends in Rhodesian politics might follow several basic directions. At one extreme is British recognition of the current regime and entrenchment of a white apartheid power structure; on the other, the total annihilation of the white elite as a political force and its replacement by Africans. Between these poles is the possibility of compromise between African and white elites in some form of cooperative government; or the current impasse might continue indefinitely. Any of these possibilities may be achieved by various means. Both fundamental causes of change and catalytic factors will have a decisive role in the nature or character of the confrontation, its magnitude, and the direction and pace of change. Contributory factors range from internal guerrilla activities to outside intervention by neighboring African states (including South Africa) or external powers such as Great Britain or the United Nations (although direct intervention by the U.N. or Britain must be discounted as an obscure possibility).

Since their arrival in Rhodesia, whites have controlled access to technology and the implements of power and have thus sustained a small minority in the face of a disenfranchised majority. This majority has never been empowered in any popular sense. Recent events suggest that continued white domination of the 95 per cent of the population who are African can only be achieved by greater use of police suppression and further discriminatory and restrictive legislation. Thus, under a situation of complete apartheid, Rhodesia would inevitably become little more than an armed camp.

The national election called by Ian Smith for July 30, 1974, resulted in yet another landslide victory for the Rhodesian Front; for the third time in a national election the RF won all fifty seats reserved for whites. Tim Gibbs, son of Sir Humphrey Gibbs, the former governor of Rhodesia, led the new Rhodesia Party as the main opposition to the RF. The RP was backed by businessmen concerned about the adverse effects of sanctions and included many followers of the Centre Party. The RP offered a more conciliatory approach to the ANC and expressed a willingness to compromise in order to achieve a settlement. It differed from the RF in degree rather than on fundamentals. Thus, for example, a statement by the RP maintained that the white role in the leadership of the country was essential but that it was opposed to discrimination and to "long-range political separation." [2] Like the Centre Party in the national election four years before, the RP polled just over 18 per cent of the votes cast,[3] thus clearly indicating the polarized nature of white Rhodesian society. Perhaps the most interesting feature of the election was the manner in which Ian Smith played down the significance of the events taking place in Mozambique. The April 25, 1974, *coup d'état* in Portugal had far-reaching consequences for Rhodesia. The change in Portuguese policy implied accelerated independence for Mozambique, which in turn could lead to increased guerrilla activity and to the exclusion of Rhodesian exports and imports from the vital ports of Beira and Lourenco Marques. Smith, however, maintained that he called the election because he felt it necessary "to reassert the authority of the government against the white 'new left.' " [4]

In the event of an African takeover, who would assume political control, and what ideological patterns would emerge? African society is far from monolithic; in fact it is highly differentiated, ranging from the chiefs to the Nationalists, from those who have been willing to work within

[2] *Christian Science Monitor,* Feb. 27, 1974.
[3] *Africa Research Bulletin,* July 1–31, 1974.
[4] *Africa,* Sept. 1974, p. 43.

the system to those who have sought its destruction. The small African elite includes a bourgeoisie, professionals such as lawyers, doctors, teachers, and religious leaders, and semiprofessionals. There is also a wide range of skilled and semiskilled urban workers,[5] and within the rural sector are different perspectives in regard to farming, capital, and a modern economy.

The Rhodesian African Nationalists have moved from system to antisystem operations, and finally to an extrasystem position of conflict. The pace of this movement has been determined primarily by the obstinacy of the white power structure. In fact, Africans have shown remarkable patience and have in many ways been forced into the current position of hostility. Direct appeals to Britain and the United Nations have led to an expectation that Rhodesian problems would be solved by external intervention rather than internal action. With channels for protest increasingly restricted, the conflict between the Rhodesian government and ZANU, ZAPU, and to some extent the ANC has become in Lewis Coser's terms, "a struggle over values and claims to scarce status, power and resources in which

[5] Urban migration is a potentially severe problem that Rhodesia will face in the future. Africans have long had urban expectations and demands. The process of urbanization has been a long and continuous one in this part of Africa. At any given time the percentage of Africans in the towns is relatively small because urban migrants are constantly coming and going. Even the rural areas can be characterized as urban-oriented. A rapid and unexpected boost to the Rhodesian economy, possibly following a settlement, could result in large-scale African migration to the cities. The Rhodesian government has had neither the resources nor the vision to plan for such an eventuality. Such a migration could produce considerable discontent and the possible emergence of an urban proletariat with new and unforeseen demands on the political system.

the aims of the opponents are to neutralize, injure or eliminate their rivals." [6] The crucial question now is how, and to what extent, the African people can be inspired with this belief.

The ZANU guerrillas have penetrated into Rhodesia's Centenary District from Mozambique, and have attacked white farms and clashed with security forces. ZANU and FRELIMO (Front for the Liberation of Mozambique), have cooperated in this venture, thus marking an alliance between African liberation movements. The guerrillas were met by a counteroffensive of Portuguese and Rhodesian troops fighting in the Zambezi Valley near the town of Tete, using Rhodesian aircraft. Meetings between Rhodesians, Portuguese, and South Africans to counter the guerrilla threat seemed to underscore once again the unity of the Southern African struggle. However, the future FRELIMO government of independent Mozambique, having fought side by side with ZANU, will no doubt favor the continuation of guerrilla activities and offer more tangible support for the struggle. Rhodesia will thus be placed in an even more vulnerable position.

The mobilization of Rhodesian forces,[7] extension of training for young white Rhodesians, and the deaths of white soldiers and of farmers have all contributed to an atmosphere of uncertainty and tension. The working to-

[6] Lewis Coser, *The Functions of Social Conflict* (Glencoe, Ill.: Free Press, 1964), p. 8.

[7] In June 1973, Rhodesia extended the existing state of emergency for another twelve months. Defense spending was also increased by 20 per cent. In February 1974 the Rhodesian government announced that it would double the national draft and recruit a second battalion of African troops. Thus was indicated the magnitude of the success of the ZANU guerrillas.

gether of ZANU and FRELIMO has been more successful than the marginal ZANU–ZAPU alliance.[8] The Centenary District is in a predominantly Shona area, and the membership of ZANU is, of course, mainly Shona. Fully aware of the implications of this threat, the Rhodesian government has authorized provincial commissioners to impose collective punishments on Shona communities that have aided guerrilla infiltrators. The commissioners have been given the discretion to act solely on the basis of suspicion; no proof is required.

The value of recent guerrilla activity lies not so much in the fact that scattered groups of guerrillas have the ability to take immediate control of Rhodesia, but rather that they have created tension within the society which might adversely affect the economic climate and bring about fear and uncertainty among white Rhodesians, as was the case in Kenya at the time of the Mau Mau prior to independence. White immigration to Rhodesia has already declined; [9] movement from tense rural areas to the cities and economic uncertainty have increased. All of this indicates qualified guerrilla success.

After many years of struggle, will the end result be a con-

[8] Most members of ZAPU are Ndebele and are based in Lusaka; thus they have more limited access to Rhodesia, than the ZANU forces.

[9] Rhodesia recorded a net gain of only 52 people through immigration in July 1973, according to the August *Monthly Digest of Statistics*. This is the lowest monthly gain since December 1968. There were 681 European immigrants in July 1973, compared with 1,136 in July 1972, and 1,171 in July 1971. European emigrants totaled 630 in July 1973, compared with 490 in July 1972 and 520 in July 1971. In the first seven months of 1973 there were 6,086 immigrants and 4,090 emigrants, leaving a net gain of 1,990 (*Rhodesia Herald*, Aug. 30, 1973).

servative African government, or will the very nature of Zimbabwean society be changed? Will the nationalist struggle merely result in a British-oriented middle-class elite that will differ only slightly from the current white elite in perspective and direction, or will a Marxist or socialist ideology alter the fabric of society? Because of the intensity of the struggle, African nationalist leaders have been preoccupied with the question of liberation, rather than with the more fundamental issue of the reordering of society after liberation. Some African leaders, both in and out of Rhodesia, have expressed a willingness to work toward a black-white *rapprochement.* With power an actuality, can it be assumed that at least some nationalists will then be willing to forego militancy for this type of multiracial participation? If there is to be a nationalist takeover, will it be by ZANU or ZAPU, or a combination of these? How would the government that would come into being under such circumstances cope with the potentially explosive problem of ethnic rivalry between the Shona and the Ndebele? None of the nationalist leaders thus far has transcended these differences.

How would a militant African government respond to the white minority? Would there be punitive actions, or reprisals against whites? Would such a government pursue a policy of Africanization? What would be the relation to South Africa, and to other parts of the White redoubt? There are few indices to provide guidelines for these questions. The alternatives open to future African rulers range from revolution to reformation, that is, the replacement of the existing power structure with minimal redrafting of the base of the society.

No matter what type of African government will come

to rule in Zimbabwe, it is clear that the country has great potential, and a settlement will no doubt be followed by economic development and vitality. It is possible to speculate that the aims and goals of a federation with labor from Malawi, mineral wealth from Zambia, and skills and directives from Zimbabwe might once again come into being, this time on African terms.

# Selected Bibliography


*Conflict and Opposition*

Boulding, Kenneth, *Conflict and Defense: A General Theory.* New York: Harper, 1962. 349p.

Coser, Lewis A. *The Functions of Social Conflict.* Glencoe, Ill.: Free Press, 1964. 188p.

Dahrandorf, Ralf. *Class and Class Conflict in Industrial Society.* Stanford: Stanford University Press, 1959. 336p.

Mack, Raymond W., and Richard C. Snyder. "The Analysis of Social Conflict—Toward an Overview and Synthesis." *Journal of Conflict Resolution,* 1, no. 2 (June 1957), 212–248.

Sartori, Giovanni. "Opposition and Control, Problems and Prospects." *Government and Opposition,* 1, no. 2 (Feb. 1966), 149–154.

Simmel, Georg. *Conflict.* Translated by Kurt H. Wolff. Glencoe, Ill.: Free Press, 1955. 195p.

*Rhodesian History and General Background*

Barber, James P. *Rhodesia: The Road to Rebellion.* New York: Published for the Institute of Race Relations by Oxford University Press, 1967. 338p.

Bowman, Larry W. *Politics in Rhodesia: White Power in an African State.* Cambridge: Harvard University Press, 1973. 206p.

Clements, Frank. *Rhodesia: The Course to Collision.* London: Pall Mall Press, 1969. 286p.

Gann, Lewis. *A History of Southern Rhodesia: Early Days to 1934.* London: Chatto and Windus, 1965. 354p.

Mason, Philip. *The Birth of a Dilemma: The Conquest and*

*Settlement of Rhodesia*. Issued under the auspices of the Institute of Race Relations. London: Oxford University Press, 1958. 366p.

Mtshali, B. Vulindlela. *Rhodesia: Background to Conflict*. New York: Hawthorn Books, 1967. 255p.

Ranger, Terence O. *The African Voice in Southern Rhodesia, 1898–1930*. London: Heinemann, 1970. 252p.

——. *Revolt in Southern Rhodesia, 1896–1897: A Study in African Resistance*. London: Heinemann, 1967. 403p.

Rea, Fred B., ed. *Southern Rhodesia: The Price of Freedom. A Series of Essays by Nine Rhodesians on the Present Political Impasse*. Bulawayo, Rhodesia: Midrho Press, 1964. 141p.

Samkange, Stanlake. *Origins of Rhodesia*. New York: Praeger, 1969. 292p.

Wills, A. J. *An Introduction to the History of Central Africa*. London: Oxford University Press, 1964. 386p.

Young, Kenneth. *Rhodesia and Independence*. New York: J. H. Heineman, 1967. 567p. Rev. ed. London: Dent, 1969. 700p.

The Central African Federation

Chidzero, Bernard T. G. *Partnership in Practice*. London: Sword of the Spirit, 1960. 30p.

Creighton, T. R. M. *The Anatomy of Partnership: Southern Rhodesia and the Central African Federation*. London: Faber and Faber, 1960. 251p.

Keatley, Patrick. *The Politics of Partnership*. Baltimore: Penguin Books, 1963. 527p.

Mason, Philip. *Year of Decision: Rhodesia and Nyasaland in 1960*. London: Oxford University Press, 1960. 282p.

Spiro, Hebert J. "The Rhodesias and Nyasaland." In *Five African States: Responses to Diversity*, edited by Gwendolen M. Carter. Ithaca, N.Y.: Cornell University Press, 1963, pp. 361–470.

Welensky, Sir Roy. *Welensky's 4000 Days: The Life and Death of the Federation of Rhodesia and Nyasaland.* New York: Roy Publishers, 1965. 383p.

1961 Constitution

Day, John. "Southern Rhodesian African Nationalists and the 1961 Constitution." *Journal of Modern African Studies,* 7 (1969), 221–247.

Dumbutshena, Enoch. "Why the Nationalists Rejected the 1961 Constitution." In *Southern Rhodesia: The Price of Freedom,* edited by Fred B. Rea. Bulawayo, Rhodesia: Midrho Press, 1964, pp. 75–90.

*The Character of Rhodesian Society*

Bull, Theodore. *Rhodesian Perspective.* London: Michael Joseph, 1967. 184p.

Clements, Frank. *Rhodesia: A Study of the Deterioration of a White Society.* New York: Praeger, 1969. 286p.

Leys, Colin. *European Politics in Southern Rhodesia.* Oxford: Clarendon Press, 1959. 323p.

Niesewand, Peter. *In Camera.* London: Weidenfeld and Nicolson, 1973.

* Peck, A. J. *Rhodesia Accuses.* Salisbury: Three Sisters, 1966. 170p.

* ——. *Rhodesia Condemns.* Salisbury: Three Sisters, 1967. 230p.

* Reed, Douglas. *The Battle for Rhodesia.* Cape Town: Haum, 1967. 172p.

Rogers, Cyril A., and C. Franz. *Racial Themes in Southern Rhodesia: The Attitudes and Behavior of the White Population.* New Haven: Yale University Press, 1962. 427p.

Todd, Judith. *The Right to Say No.* Stanford, Calif.: Third Press, 1973. 200p.

* Apologists for the white system.

The Church in Rhodesia

*Rhodesia, the Moral Issue: Pastoral Letters of the Catholic Bishops.* Gwelo, Rhodesia: Mambo Press, 1968. 108p.

Salisbury Archdiocese. *Peace through Justice: Pastoral Instruction of the Catholic Bishops of Southern Rhodesia.* Gwelo, Rhodesia: Catholic Mission Press, 1961.

Sithole, Ndabaningi. "The Interaction of Christianity and African Political Development." In *Historians in Tropical Africa: Proceedings of the Leverhulme Inter-Collegiate History Conference,* edited by D. P. Abraham. Salisbury: University College of Rhodesia and Nyasaland, 1962, pp. 351–364.

——. *Obed Mutezo: The Mudzimu Christian Nationalist.* New York: Oxford University Press, 1971. 210p.

Townsend, H. G. *As We Are One: The Christian in a Plural Society.* Gwelo, Rhodesia: Catholic Mission Press, 1962. 120p.

*Traditional Society and the Chiefs*

Aquina, Sister Mary [A. K. H. Weinrich]. *Chiefs and Councils in Rhodesia: Transition from Patriarchal to Bureaucratic Power.* London: Heinemann, 1971. 252p. United States ed. Columbia: University of South Carolina Press, 1971.

Holleman, J. F. *Chief Council and Commissioner: Some Problems of Government in Rhodesia.* London: Oxford University Press, 1969. 391p. Published on behalf of the Afrika-Studiecentrum by Royal VanGorcum, Assen, The Netherlands.

Kuper, Hilda. *The Shona and Ndebele of Southern Rhodesia.* London: International African Institute, 1954. 131p.

Rayner, William. *The Tribe and Its Successors: An Account of African Traditional Life and European Settlement in Southern Rhodesia.* New York: Praeger, 1962. 239p.

## *African Nationalism*

Gibson, Richard. *African Liberation Movements: Contemporary Struggles against White Minority Rule.* London: Published for the Institute of Race Relations by Oxford University Press, 1972. 350p.

Mlambo, Eshmael Ephial Mtshumayeli. *Rhodesia: The Struggle for a Birthright.* London: C. Hurst, 1972. 333p.

† Morris, Michael. *Terrorism: The First Full Account in Detail of Terrorism and Insurgency in Southern Africa.* Cape Town: Timmins, 1971. 249p.

Nkomo, Joshua. "The Case for Majority Rule in Southern Rhodesia." *Africa Quarterly,* 4, no. 2 (July/Sept. 1964), 91–101.

Shamuyarira, Nathan M. *Crisis in Rhodesia.* London: Andre Deutsch, 1965. 240p.

Sithole, Ndabaningi. *African Nationalism.* 2d ed. London: Oxford University Press, 1968. 196p.

Van Velsen, J. "Trends in African Nationalism in Southern Rhodesia." *Kroniek van Afrika,* 2 (June 1964).

† Venter, A. L. J. *The Terror Fighter: A Profile of Guerrilla Warfare in Southern Africa.* Cape Town: Purnell, 1969. 152p.

## *Constitutional and Legal Documents*

Great Britain, Foreign and Commonwealth Office. *Rhodesia: Documents Relating to Proposals for a Settlement, 1966* (cmnd. 3171). London: H.M.S.O., 1966. 103p.

——, Foreign and Commonwealth Office. *Rhodesia: Report of the Commission on Rhodesian Opinion under the Chairmanship of the Right Honourable Lord Pearce* (cmnd. 4964). London: H.M.S.O., 1972. 212p.

——, Foreign and Commonwealth Office. *Rhodesia: Proposals*


† The term "terrorism" is most frequently used by those who oppose meaningful African political aspirations in Southern Africa.

*for a Settlement, 1966* (cmnd. 3159). London: H.M.S.O., 1966. 12p.

——, Foreign and Commonwealth Office. *Rhodesia: Proposals for a Settlement, with Correction Slip* (cmnd. 4835). London: H.M.S.O., 1971. 40p.

——, Foreign and Commonwealth Office. *Rhodesia: Report of Exchanges with the Regime since the Talks Held in Salisbury in November, 1968* (cmnd. 4065). London: H.M.S.O., 1968. 32p.

——, Foreign and Commonwealth Office. *Southern Rhodesia: Documents Relating to the Negotiations between the United Kingdom and the Southern Rhodesian Governments, November, 1963–November, 1965* (cmnd. 2807). London: H.M.S.O., 1965. 142p.

——, Foreign and Commonwealth Office, Library. *Southern Rhodesia: The Illegal Declaration of Independence.* 2d ed. London: H.M.S.O., 1968. 26p.

——, House of Commons, Bills, Session 1969–1970. *Rhodesia: Independence.* London: H.M.S.O., 1968. 2p.

——, Prime Minister and Secretary of State for Commonwealth Affairs. *Rhodesia: Report on the Discussions held on board H.M.S. Fearless, October, 1968* (cmnd. 3793). London: H.M.S.O., 1968. 12p.

Palley, Claire. *The Constitutional History and Law of Southern Rhodesia, 1888–1965, with Special Reference to Imperial Control.* Oxford: Clarendon Press, 1966. 872p.

Passmore, Gloria C. *Local Government Legislation in Southern Rhodesia up to 30th September, 1963.* Salisbury: University College of Rhodesia and Nyasaland, Department of Government, 1966. 65p.

——, and M. T. Mitchell. *Source-Book of Parliamentary Elections and Referenda in Southern Rhodesia, 1898–1962.* Salisbury: University College of Rhodesia and Nyasaland, Department of Government, 1963. 255p.

Rhodesia. *The Domboshawa "Indaba": The Demand for Independence in Rhodesia (Consultation with the African Tribesmen through Their Chiefs and Headmen*). Salisbury: Government Printer, 1964. 61p.

——. "The Rhodesian Constitution (Verbatim)." *African Scholar*, 1, no. 4 (1970), 21–32.

——, Constitutional Council. *Report for 1968*. Salisbury: Government Printer, 1969. 12p.

——, Parliament, Prime Minister. *Anglo-Rhodesian Relations: Proposals for a Settlement. Presented to Parliament by the Prime Minister on 25th November, 1971, CRR 46, 1971*. Salisbury: Government Printer, 1971. 37p.

Southern Rhodesia. *Proposals for a New Constitution for Rhodesia* (CSR 32). Salisbury: Government Printer, 1969. 21p.

——. *The African Affairs Act, Chapter 92, 1928*. Salisbury: Government Printer, 1928. 17p.

——. *The Council of Chiefs and Provincial Assemblies Act, Chapter 111, 1961*. Salisbury: Government Printer, 1961. 5p. and Amendments.

Southern Rhodesian Constitutional Conference (Salisbury, 1961). *Report* (cmnd. 1291). London: H.M.S.O., 1961. 9p.

## *Newspapers*

*African Times*. Salisbury: Government Printer.

*Battle Cry*. Salisbury: Zimbabwe African National Union of Southern Rhodesia.

*Central Africa Examiner*. Salisbury.

*Chapupu*. Salisbury: African National Congress.

*Citizen*. Salisbury. (A right-wing white weekly.)

*Daily News*. Salisbury. (An African publication, banned in 1964.)

*Democratic Voice*. Salisbury: National Democratic Party.

*Evening Standard*. Salisbury.

*Moto*. Gwelo, Rhodesia: Mambo Press, 1966–1970. (Catholic.)

*Rhodesian Commentary*. Salisbury: Government Printer.

*Rhodesia Herald*. Salisbury.

*Shield*. Published by the Catholic Church in Salisbury.

*Spear*. Published by the Zimbabwe African People's Union.

*Sunday Mail*. Salisbury.

*ZANU News*. First published in Salisbury, later in Dar-es-Salaam, Tanzania, by the Zimbabwe African National Union.

*Zimbabwe News*. Dar-es-Salaam and Lusaka, Zambia: Zimbabwe African National Union.

*Zimbabwe Review*. Lusaka and Cairo: Zimbabwe African People's Union.

# Index